ENDORSEMENTS

Christine Fisher, a well-seasoned writer, has captured glimpses of God's glory, not only in her previous books but also in this book, *God's Glory Manifested*. She has shown how we identify God's glory in each other as we are made in His image and how we show love for each other, thus spreading the glory. Through her knowledge of the Old Testament, Christine shows us how God reveals His glory primarily through His actions and laws, which indicate His power and presence among us. She continues this revelation in the New Testament as she focuses on the glory of God that is made visible in Jesus Christ, who she describes as the radiance of God's glory manifested and the exact representation of His being. For those who need an uplifting look at our world and the God who created it, *God's Glory Manifested* is an ideal way to experience it.

Gary DiLallo
Brigadier General (Ret) US Army Reserves

Christine sees God's glory manifested in big and small life events, and even in the most difficult of times. She challenges us to see our situations through the lens of our faith, and to never lose sight of the wonders of God. She asks those spiritual questions which make us 'ponder' our own personal connection to our Lord through nature, people, and Scripture. Whether we are young, old, a new Christian, or just looking for a fresh perspective, this devotional will surely bless all who open its cover. After all, nothing happens by chance!

Carol Palmiter
Friend and Sister in Christ

Christine's writings show us simple ways to make a positive difference in our own lives, the lives of others, and today's troubled world. Today's world needs positive Christian influences. As more people read Christine's books and visit her website, hopetoinspireyou.com, all the more lives will be changed for the better. Then perhaps they, too, will be inspired to share her writings with others. I envision this having a "flooding" effect or spreading like wildfire! Christine "hopes to inspire you" and she succeeds. I, in turn, hope to inspire others by sharing how I have been blessed and inspired by her books and website. I am looking forward to her fourth book, *God's Glory Manifested!*

Lynn Graham
Friend and Soul Sister

Christine Fisher is one who not only sees God all around her as she walks her journey of faith, but in her books, she shares glimpses of God, that we might see better His presence in our lives, each other, and nature. Her words illuminate our hearts and minds to focus more closely on God. *God's Glory Manifested* will bring the reader to the summit of seeing God's glory all around. Each page promises to transform the reader's understanding of where and how to experience His glory deeper within their own lives.

Michael R. Stanistreet
Follower of Christ

Other books by Christine M. Fisher:

God's Presence Illuminated:
Treasured Thoughts to Inspire Hope and Light

God's Love Illuminated:
Treasured Thoughts to Inspire Walking in God's Abundant Love
Winner, 2023 Christian Literary Awards
Henri Award
Receiving the Seal of Excellence Medallion

God's Compassion Illuminated:
Treasured Thoughts to Inspire Following God's Way
Finalist, 2024 Christian Literary Awards
Henri Award, Devotional & Inspirational Categories
Receiving the Seal of Excellence Medallion

GOD'S GLORY MANIFESTED

Treasured Thoughts to Inspire the Experience of God's Presence

A 90-DAY DEVOTIONAL

CHRISTINE M. FISHER

God's Glory Manifested
Treasured Thoughts to Inspire
the Experience of God's Presence
Christine M. Fisher

To contact the author:
christine@hopetoinspireyou.com
www.hopetoinspireyou.com

Published by:

Mary Ethel

Mary Ethel Eckard
Frisco, Texas

Library of Congress Catalog Number: 2024907734
ISBN (Print): 979-8-9894822-7-6
ISBN (E-book): 979-8-9894822-8-3

Cover photo by Christine M. Fisher, 2023
Location: Lake Ontario at Stony Point, Henderson, NY

CONTENTS

Dedication xi

Foreword.. xiii

Introduction..xix

SECTION 1: GOD'S GLORY MANIFESTED IN NATURE 1

1. Praise and Glory.. 3
2. Windy Effects 6
3. Son Rise 10
4. The Seed 15
5. Rough Waters 16
6. Silence is Golden 19
7. Faith and Trust 22
8. Slow Down 26
9. Step by Step 28
10. Little Day Brighteners 32
11. Water Reminders... 36
12. Great Love 41
13. Holy Ground 44
14. The Cedar Tree 47
15. Everyday Miracles 53
16. The Vast Ocean 56
17. Everything Changes 58
18. Beautiful Blessing.. 62

19. Butterflies 66

20. Resilient 70

21. Always With You 73

22. GPS Saga 75

23. Calm Waters 77

24. The Pearl 80

25. In Awe 83

26. Come Away With Me 86

27. Uncharted Waters 89

28. Fall Time Beauty 91

29. Advice From a Tree 95

SECTION 2: GOD'S GLORY MANIFESTED IN PEOPLE 101

30. Amazing Things 103

31. Priorities 107

32. God's Purposes 110

33. Restoration 113

34. Spread A Little Kindness 117

35. The Simple Things 119

36. Hidden Treasures 123

37. Rise Above 125

38. Moment by Moment 129

39. Graduation 130

40. A Time of Refreshment 134

41. Your Words are Influential 137

42. Strength In Unity 139

43. God's Orchestrations 142

44. The Cheerleaders 145

45. Precious Angel 148

46. Value Opportunities 150

47. An 8–Minute Challenge 155

48. The Little Details 158

49. Joyous Oneness 160

50. Bucket List.. 164

51. The Blessing of People................................167

52. Living Well 169

53. Painful Times 173

54. Life Lessons..176

55. Spiritual Gratitude 180

56. Joyful Expectation......................................184

57. Lasting Impressions.................................... 187

58. Right Timing..191

59. Growing in Love 195

60. Stranger Blessings.......................................198

SECTION 3: GOD'S GLORY MANIFESTED IN JESUS..........203

61. Glorified Body 205

62. Worship 211

63. Servanthood...213

64. Sacrifice 215

65. There is Hope 219

66. Marvel 221

67. Ministry Reflections 227

68. Jesus' Presence... 230

69. True Friends... 234

70. God's Promises... 236

71. Our Supernatural God................................. 241

72. Easter Joy 245

73. Postures of Worship 247

74. God's Breath 253

75. The Light 256

76. Foot Washing..259

77. Martha or Mary 263

78. Time to Be With Him 266

79. Praise to Him 270

80. The Gift of Presence 272

81. The Body of Christ 276

82. Tragedies 281

83. Resurrection 285

84. The Vision 289

85. The Lord's Prayer 290

86. Obedient Growth 294

87. September Reflections 298

88. The Face of Jesus 302

89. The Kingdom of Heaven 306

90. Prism of Light 310

Conclusion 315

About the Author 317

Notes 319

DEDICATION

This labor of love is dedicated first to God, who, in His infinite love, reveals His glory in all aspects of creation. What a privilege to witness the manifestation of God's glory everywhere and every day.

It is also dedicated to the beautiful people who love, support, and encourage my writing journey. I have grown so much since 2014 when I started sharing weekly reflections on my website, hopetoinspireyou.com. Thank you for being part of my spiritual family. You are a blessing, and I am forever grateful for the impact of your life on mine as we journey in faith together.

God bless!

"All your works praise you, Lord; your faithful people extol you. They tell of the glory of your kingdom and speak of your might, so that all people may know of your mighty acts and the glorious splendor of your kingdom."
~ Psalm 145:10-12

FOREWORD

Time is a gift from God. It keeps everything
from happening at once.

"Hello, you don't know me, but I think God wants me to give you this book. My name is Christine Fisher, and I am an author."

Pause… Pause…

"Thank you," I said, wondering to myself why me and who is this author. I never heard of her, but her name was on the book cover. And so, on Thursday evening, February 9, 2023, Christine Fisher came into my life and presented me with her newest book, *God's Compassion Illuminated* – a 90-day devotional.

Doesn't everyone have this experience in life; a complete stranger intersects your life and says I have a message for you from God? And so began, as of this writing for the Foreword for Christine's fourth and newest book, *God's Glory Manifested*, a one-year spirit-filled journey with this gifted author.

God's Orchestration

A month prior to meeting Christine, I read about an upcoming weekly video series, "Metanoia," with Father David Pivonka, at Our Lady of Good Counsel Church near Binghamton, NY. My wife and I were visiting family in the area for three weeks and I thought, why not, sounds like a good spiritual opportunity for me.

At the conclusion of each night's video series, there was an opportunity to offer prayer intentions. I stood and asked prayers for safe travels the next day to an out-of-town funeral for a dear friend, the repose of his soul, and healing for his family. And then I asked for a second prayer intention for my wife and I as we planned to drive back home to Florida after the funeral.

Christine approached me after the meeting closed and shared with me that she brought a copy of her book to the meeting and an inquisitive person at her table asked who the book was for; she did not know. After my prayer intentions, she heard God's voice say, "Give him the book."

We conversed for a good forty minutes. Christine described herself as an introvert and ordinary gal and she was every bit an introvert in the initial encounter on that snowy February night in upstate NY. Our discussion centered around family, God, faith, religion, and our individual pilgrimages to Israel. I learned about her love for pre-mature babies in the NICU, her love for prayer, and her love in serving others at soup kitchens. I learned that Christine began her writing career in the early 1970s through journaling and other writings. It was these early writings that began her formation and, after many years, resulted in publishing her first book *God's Presence Illuminated* in October 2020.

Christine shared her faith in a very quiet spiritual manner that night. It wasn't self-seeking for her accomplishments, and it wasn't inward focused about her personally. My instinct was telling me she wanted to share so much more about her faith and her shyness presented me the chance to ask questions to discover more about her faith journey. I could tell there was depth beyond the shyness. Soon I needed to leave and I left thinking the video series was uplifting, and oh, nice, that is cool, I met an author.

Back to Florida and into my professional work life and Church routines, I began reading Christine's book, *God's Compassion Illuminated*, and quickly was absorbed into the daily devotionals. I was very much drawn into her writing style of using short Bible verses intermixed with her personal stories and reflection questions which led me further into the deeper waters of our faith. The open-ended reflection questions especially made me reflect about my personal faith journey in ways I had not previously engaged in and caused me to be become more introspective of my faith and beliefs. Christine makes her writing very easy to read, using all the senses to take you deeper in your faith journey.

I also signed up to receive Christine's weekly devotionals, from her website: hopetoinspireyou.com and, again, reflection questions designed to strengthen our relationship with the Lord. I highly encourage you, the reader, if you have not done so, to pick up copies of Christine's other three books and sign up for her website.

> *"The will of God will never take you where the*
> *grace of God cannot sustain you."*
> ~ Billy Graham

I never expected that after God's forty-minute orchestration in February, the spiritual journey would continue with Christine. I have had the privilege and pleasure to continue interactions with Christine over the past 52 weeks through text messages and occasional phone calls.

Soon after my return to Florida, Christine contacted me, excited, but a bit nervous about an upcoming opportunity for her to speak for 20-25 minutes with reflections from her recent new book at a monthly meeting of a local organization. For many of us, talking in front of a group for that extended time can be challenging; to an introvert, I am sure it can be daunting. We prayed about the opportunity and how God was using her to reach others. I offered to be a sounding board for her to do a practice run or two to build up her confidence. This happened a few more times as Christine was asked to speak to other organizational groups which varied in size and interest areas. Over time, as Christine gained self-assurance and allowed God's graces to work through her, I could hear in her voice the confidence growing and her ability to deliver a well-received message.

As I witness God's gifts manifested in Christine, I am reminded of a recent Gospel reading at Mass from Mark 4:26-33. Jesus tells an interesting parable about seed scattered on the land, which yields fruit in a manner unknown to the farmer. God's grace is at work growing inside each of us; even when we are unaware of it and even when we feel lost or inept. God never abandons us to our own weaknesses. Our lives bear fruit because of grace, which is sown patiently over time. This was evident to me as I witnessed Christine stepping out in faith and growing.

God will meet you where you are and take you where He wants you to be. Where was God taking Christine?

<u>God does not call the equipped, He equips those He calls.</u>

In September, unaware that someone had given her name to "Women Living Well Ministries," Christine was contacted by the ministry to see if she would be interested in applying for a new position on their team. In Christine's words she shared with me, "they are looking for gifted teachers to teach and write articles to disciples. I don't think I am qualified." She started the paperwork, interview process, and produced her first three-minute teaching video for submission. In late November, Christine was offered a position with the "Women Living Well Ministries," that would also entail producing a series of five-minute videos that would be used to teach disciples. Being able to deliver a succinct, clear, and focused message can be as challenging, if not more, than a twenty minute talk. A few more phone calls with Christine, a few five minute practice talks, and by mid-January 2024 she produced her first go-live video for the ministry.

I have come to be a firm believer that there are no coincidences in this life, only God's orchestration in bringing people into our lives to take us where He wants us.

In one short year, I have had the privilege of walking this journey with Christine and have seen first-hand God's amazing work in Christine's life by her openness to being led by God and trusting in His plan. Many times, spiritual growth can be painful as it takes us outside our comfort zone. God is in control and has a plan for our lives, even when we don't see it. If God is your co-pilot, switch seats.

Each of us is being called by God to do His will. May we, like Christine, allow God to do things through us, rather than us doing things for God.

We have each been put on this earth at this exact time, in this particular place, for a specific mission from God that only we can complete. May each of us have an encounter with the risen Christ, a deep-continuous faith conversion, resulting in a new life in Christ.

Christine's mission is to bring a deeper awareness of God's love, presence, and compassion to us through her writings. In her newest book, *God's Glory Manifested,* may Christine's writing continue to inspire and lead all of us to an even deeper awareness of God's glory present and working in our lives.

John Fazio
Spiritual Brother

INTRODUCTION

"For everything comes from him and exists by his power
and is intended for his glory. All glory to him forever! Amen."
~ Romans 11:36 (NLT)

As I follow God's path with my writing and speaking ministry, the theme of God's glory continues to resonate with my heart, sparking a desire to share it through the written word. From a Google search using the Oxford Languages Dictionary, a definition for the word *glory* is "magnificence or great beauty." Baker's Evangelical Dictionary of Biblical Theology defines *God's glory* as "the external manifestation of His being." I view God's glory as God's magnificence, or great beauty, that we see and experience on this earth. God's glory continually appears, is revealed, and can be seen.

> Out of nothing, He made everything, the eternal manifestation of His being, creating magnificence and great beauty.

When we think back to the story of creation, when God created the heavens and the earth and filled the earth with different masterpieces each day, including Adam and Eve, we recognize God's glory. Out of nothing, He made everything, the external manifestation of His being, creating magnificence and great beauty. Everything was just as glorious and perfect as God intended it to be.

When Adam and Eve disobeyed God and ate from the tree of knowledge, sin entered the world. No longer was God's glory His alone. Sin is us, thinking we know best and wanting to be in control, working to shift the glory to us. Glory should be God's alone, and our hope is found in God's plan of sending Jesus to earth to die for our sin. By accepting Jesus as our Lord and Savior, God's glory invades our lives, and we are rescued from our sin.

Manifestations of God's glory are revealed to us every day when we see with our spiritual eyes. This fascinates me and holds me in awe of our Creator. All the nature that God created bears witness to His glory. Did you know that God's glory is also present in every person He creates? You, my reader, reveal God's glory to everyone who knows you. Jesus is the perfect representative of God's glory. Jesus obediently went to the cross for you and for me so that God's presence could be manifested in all of humanity.

I pray that as you read these reflections, you may experience God's glory that is revealed all around us. May the ending Scripture for each reflection, which contains a version of the word glory, give you reason to praise God for His manifestations of glory.

Be assured that God's glory is alive, powerful, and close to us. It is one of the greatest gifts He blesses us with. May the Spirit give you spiritual eyes to see how all creation manifests God's glory.

God's glory manifested.

> *"I can't do big things. But I want all I do, even the*
> *smallest thing, to be for the greater glory of God."*
> ~ St. Dominic Savio

Section 1

GOD'S GLORY
MANIFESTED
IN NATURE

"Yahweh now reigns as King! Let everyone rejoice! His rule extends everywhere, even to distant lands, and the islands of the sea, let them all be glad. Clouds both dark and mysterious now surround him. His throne of glory rests upon a foundation of righteousness and justice. All around him burns a blazing glory-fire consuming all his foes. When his lightning strikes, it lights up the world. People are wide-eyed as they tremble and shake. Mountains melt away like wax in a fire when the Lord of all the earth draws near. Heaven's messengers preach righteousness, and people everywhere see God's glory in the sky!"
~ Psalm 97:1-6 (TPT)

In the beginning, God created the heavens and the earth. We learn from Scripture that the earth was formless and empty, with darkness over the surface of the deep. The Spirit of God hovering over the waters began God's creation of what we behold on the earth today: the light, the sky, the vegetation, the trees, the birds, the livestock, man, woman, and more. All of nature displays the manifestation of God's presence, whether it is the beauty found in viewing the creation or the purpose that it serves.

Manifestations of God's glory surround us throughout the nature that He created. The sky is one of the most powerful places where we can be in God's presence while viewing a sunrise, a sunset, a rainbow, the hot summer sun, a lightning storm, or peaceful snow falling.

God's glory manifested in nature.

"I love to think of nature as an unlimited broadcasting station, through which God speaks to us every hour, if we will only tune in."
~ George Washington Carver

Christine M. Fisher

1

Praise and Glory

A little bit of heaven on earth.

How does that sound to you?

Don't we often think about how, when we are in heaven, we will be with the Lord forever and always praise Him?

How about if we tried doing more of that very thing, praising Him?

Have you thought about and reflected on the fact that God created **all** of creation and meant for us to continually give praise and glory to Him?

Shouldn't everything give glory to the Creator?

Do you strive to live this way every day even though bad things happen, or things do not go according to your plans? It is so important to continually praise the Lord through **all** that happens.

Take a few minutes to reflect on these words:

> *"For you love all things that are and loathe nothing that you have made; for you would not fashion what you hate. How could a thing remain, unless you willed it; or be preserved, had it not been called forth by you? But you spare all things, because they are yours. O Ruler and Lover of souls, for your imperishable spirit is in all things!"*
> ~ Wisdom 11:24-26 (NABRE)

Aren't those words powerful?

Look around. What do you see?

The sky, flowers, animals, insects, waters, stars, and leaves that change colors and fall off the trees; the list goes on and on.

If we agree that the Lord God made everything we see, we know it remains because He wills it.

Why do the stars appear every night?
> Why do the leaves turn colors in autumn and fall to the earth?
>> Why do the geese fly south, and the clouds bring snow in the winter?

All because the Lord wills it, and it has been called forth by Him. All these creations are giving praise to their Creator by fulfilling the Lord's purpose for them.

Now turn your thoughts to people, God's greatest creation, made in His image. I like this story that highlights Zacchaeus' readiness to give praise to Jesus.

> *"When Jesus reached the spot, He looked up and said to him, 'Zacchaeus, come down immediately. I must stay at your house today.' So he came down at once and welcomed him gladly. Jesus said to him, 'Today salvation has come to this house, because this man, too, is a son of Abraham. For the Son of Man came to seek and to save the lost.'"*
> ~ Luke 19:5-6, 9-10

God gave us humans free will, something that all other creation does not have. Jesus waits patiently for all His children to come to the point where they praise Him in their lives.

It is interesting to see that Jesus had this urgency and foresight that the time was right for Zacchaeus to praise his Creator. Zacchaeus, hearing that Jesus was passing by, climbed a sycamore tree, as he was too short to see Jesus amidst the crowd of people. Jesus knew Zacchaeus' heart and actively sought him out to stay at his house that evening. What a great visit that must have been. From that point on, Zacchaeus served the Lord with joy and praise.

As humans, don't we find it harder to praise the Lord during difficult times, especially when suffering from things of this world, like sickness and death?

I challenge you to continually praise and give glory to God. Yes, even during difficult times. God is our sovereign Lord, and all of creation was made to give Him praise and glory.

REFLECTION:

Can you think of a time you made a conscious effort to give glory to God despite difficult circumstances?
How have you seen creation give God the glory due to Him?

"Worthy are you, our Lord and God, to receive glory and honor and power, for you created all things, and by your will they existed and were created."
~ Revelation 4:11 (ESV)

2

Windy Effects

It was intriguing as I observed the water at Lake Ontario for a few days to see how the wind affected the water. On some days, I noticed that the wind caused slight ripples on the water, which made it go to the right, and other days the wind caused the water to go to the left.

Isn't the wind interesting? We cannot see the wind, yet we can sometimes see, feel, or hear its effects. At times, the wind can produce negative effects, such as the devastation caused by hurricanes. Other times, the wind can have a positive effect, like a gentle breeze on a summer day that cools and refreshes our skin.

Seeing the effect of the wind made me reflect on some parallels with God and our lives. Just like we observe in life, sometimes the wind is portrayed negatively in the Bible and sometimes positively. In Scripture, the wind, especially the positive aspects of it, is symbolic of the Holy Spirit.

As you read the following passages, take time to reflect on the significance of the Holy Spirit as a representative of the wind. What does Scripture tell us about the wind?

"You [God] are dressed in a robe of light. You stretch out the starry curtain of the heavens; you lay out the rafters of your home in the rain clouds. You make the clouds your chariot; you ride upon the wings of the wind. The winds are your messengers; flames of fire are your servants."
~ Psalm 104:2-4 (NLT)

We learn from this psalm that God has a purpose for everything in the heavens. The wind that blows where He wills it contains messages of God's great power and love. God has a purpose for everything in His creation.

> *"Praise the Lord from the earth, you great sea creatures and all deeps,*
> *fire and hail, snow and mist, stormy wind fulfilling his word!"*
> ~ Psalm 148:7-8 (ESV)

What a great psalm of praise showing that even the earth and all the elements of the weather fulfill God's Word. All of creation that God made glorifies their Creator.

> *"The Lord does whatever pleases him throughout all heaven*
> *and earth, and on the seas and in their depths. He causes the*
> *clouds to rise over the whole earth. He sends the lightning with*
> *the rain and releases the wind from his storehouses."*
> ~ Psalm 135:6-7 (NLT)

What a powerful message the psalmist shares about the magnitude of the Lord's dominion. God has complete sovereignty over all of heaven, earth, the seas, the skies, and everything. The wind comes and goes at the Lord's command.

How did God use the wind in Scripture to accomplish His purposes?

> *"But God remembered Noah and all the wild animals and*
> *livestock with him in the boat. He sent a wind to blow across*
> *the earth, and the floodwaters began to recede."*
> ~ Genesis 8:1 (NLT)

In the beginning, God destroyed the earth by sending a flood for forty days, followed by another hundred and fifty days before the waters receded. Only Noah, his family, and the animals were kept safe in the ark Noah built as God had instructed. What made the floodwaters begin to recede? It was the wind God sent to blow across the earth. Indeed, even the winds fulfill God's purposes for His glory.

> *"Then Moses stretched out his hand over the sea, and the*
> *Lord drove the sea back by a strong east wind all night and*
> *made the sea dry land, and the waters were divided."*
> ~ Exodus 14:21 (ESV)

When Moses was leading the Israelites into the Promised Land, trying to get away from the Egyptians, God sent a strong east wind all night, which made the sea dry up and divide. The Israelites crossed the sea safely, but the waters came back together as the Egyptians were crossing.

> *"When the day of Pentecost came, they were all together in one place.*
> *Suddenly a sound like the blowing of a violent wind came from*
> *heaven and filled the whole house where they were sitting. They saw*
> *what seemed to be tongues of fire that separated and came to rest*
> *on each of them. All of them were filled with the Holy Spirit and*
> *began to speak in other tongues as the Spirit enabled them."*
> ~ Acts 2:1-4

After Jesus died and was resurrected, He returned and walked this earth for another forty days. Then He ascended into heaven where He sits at the right hand of God. Ten days later, the apostles were in a locked room when God used the sound of a violent wind to fill them with the Holy Spirit, which was Pentecost.

Be encouraged to remember that the wind, both earthly and in our lives…

is under God's reign.
teaches us about God.
fulfills God's Word and purposes.

Christine M. Fisher

May the wind of the Holy Spirit in your life accomplish God's purposes.

REFLECTION:

What is one way you have experienced the wind of the Holy Spirit in your life?

How has the Spirit used you to be the wind in someone's life?

"So they shall fear the name of the Lord from the west, and his glory from the rising of the sun; for he will come like a rushing stream, which the wind of the Lord drives."
~ Isaiah 59:19 (ESV)

3

Son Rise

With the days growing shorter as winter approached, I experienced a glorious sunrise and sunset on the same day while at a retreat on Canandaigua Lake, which is one of my holy places. I am more of a night owl than an early riser, so noting that the sunrise was around 7:30 a.m. inspired me to get up a little earlier. This was the first time I had a room with a lakeside view, so when I awoke, I was greeted with the horizon bursting with red and orange color before the sun rose. Naturally, I had to go outside to get a better view, feeling united with God and the beauty.

I enjoyed the quiet, still atmosphere of being alone in the grassy field overlooking the lake—just God and me. It was a sacred time, watching the horizon in expectation as the sun came up. I wondered what specifically the Scripture said that contained the words, *"From the rising of the sun to the place where it sets."*

> *"Praise the Lord. Praise the Lord, you his servants; praise the name of the Lord. Let the name of the Lord be praised, both now and forevermore. From the rising of the sun to the place where it sets, the name of the Lord is to be praised. The Lord is exalted over all the nations, his glory above the heavens. Who is like the Lord our God, the One who sits enthroned on high, who stoops down to look on the heavens and the earth?"*
> ~ Psalm 113:1-6

What a wonderful reminder for us. One of our primary purposes is to praise the Lord all day long, from the rising of the sun to its setting. Think for a few minutes about the goodness of God in your life. The Lord made everything for us to enjoy. He made you and me in His image to love as He does. His glory is found everywhere. He loves and cares for each one of us.

"Those who live at the ends of the earth stand in awe of your wonders. From where the sun rises to where it sets, you inspire shouts of joy."
~ Psalm 65:8 (NLT)

Are you in awe of God's ways that are above ours?

Do you see how He brings people into your life, even if for a season, that impact your life for the better?

When you see the wonders of our God working everything out for your good, doesn't it bring you such joy that you want to share it with everyone you meet?

"For from the rising of the sun to its setting my name will be great among the nations, and in every place incense will be offered to my name, and a pure offering. For my name will be great among the nations, says the Lord of hosts."
~ Malachi 1:11 (ESV)

God's name has always been intended to be great among the nations. All day long, from the rising of the sun until its setting, God is to be praised. *Incense and offering* in this verse can also be interpreted as *prayer and praise*, respectively. Does your life continually reflect that?

After viewing the sunrise, I went inside for morning prayer. As we were praying and praising the Lord, I saw the sunrise come through the chapel window. I was in awe of the beautiful glow that shone forth, reminding me of God's spirit illuminating the chapel and us all. I couldn't help but think the sight was symbolic of the Malachi verse.

As the sun appeared in the sky, made its ascent, and illuminated the sky, my prayer was that "the Son [Jesus] would arise more and more in my life." In fact, I took a picture of my shadow as I turned to go back inside. It symbolized for me the Son, Jesus, filling me and reflecting in me, which is my heart's desire.

"These are the last words of David: 'David, the son of Jesse, speaks—David, the man who was raised up so high, David, the man anointed by the God of Jacob, David, the sweet psalmist of Israel. The Spirit of the Lord speaks through me; his words are upon my tongue. The God of Israel spoke. The Rock of Israel said to me: "The one who rules righteously, who rules in the fear of God, is like the light of morning at sunrise, like a morning without clouds, like the gleaming of the sun on new grass after rain.""
~ 2 Samuel 23:1-4 (NLT)

We are like the sunrise, shining brightly when we strive to live righteously, obediently following God's ways, and being in awe of Him. May our prayer always be to have the Lord's spirit speak through us as He leads and directs our words and actions. It is a privilege to share God's Word and love with others.

"The Lord is my light and my salvation—so why should I be afraid? The Lord is my fortress, protecting me from danger, so why should I tremble? When evil people come to devour me, when my enemies and foes attack me, they will stumble and fall. Though a mighty army surrounds me, my heart will not be afraid. Even if I am attacked, I will remain confident. The one thing I ask of the Lord—the thing I seek most—is to live in the house of the Lord all the days of my life, delighting in the Lord's perfections and meditating in his Temple."
~ Psalm 27:1-4 (NLT)

As I watched the sunrise, I thought about how the Lord is symbolic of the sun. Yes, the Lord is that light in our lives. He is our light and salvation.

Christine M. Fisher

We should not be afraid because His light is leading and shining in our lives. We need to be confident, knowing that through everything, God is working it all out for our best. Our heart's desire should be to continually dwell as one with the Lord, delighting in His goodness while praising Him.

It was a full-circle moment to experience God's presence in both the sunrise and sunset. From the rising of the sun to its setting, it was a wonderful day filled with His beauty in nature, as well as His presence and orchestrations throughout the retreat.

It was a God moment for me to receive a sunset picture the next day from a friend. It is from another holy place of mine, at Lake Ontario. It took my breath away to look at the beauty. I couldn't help but be in awe of seeing how beautifully the sunset colors were reflected upon the water. May our lives glow like the water as we radiate God's beauty that shines forth from us.

As the water reflects the sunset, may our lives radiate God's beauty.

Be encouraged to...

> praise the Lord from the rising of the sun to the place it sets.
> be in awe of the wonders of God, inspiring you to shout out in joy.
> pray that the Son will arise more and more in your life.
> shine like the sun as you live in obedience and righteousness.
> know that the Lord, the light, is leading you as you seek and delight in Him.

REFLECTION:

Can you praise the Lord today from the rising of the sun until its setting? How can you intentionally radiate God's beauty to someone today?

"There are heavenly bodies and earthly bodies, but the glory of the heavenly is of one kind, and the glory of the earthly is of another. There is one glory of the sun, and another glory of the moon, and another glory of the stars; for star differs from star in glory."
~ 1 Corinthians 15:40-41 (ESV)

Christine M. Fisher

4

The Seed

Our lives can be parallel to those of a little, tiny seed. The seed is just being planted in the dirt when we realize the true purpose and meaning of life—life in Jesus Christ.

The growth of the seed will continue when we read and share God's Word and reach out to one another. These are the water and food that nourish the seed.

In reaching out to others, we help ourselves grow as well as bring others to know and love Jesus more. This is the sun, and when it shines brightly, it helps the seed blossom into something beautiful.

At times, clouds and storms may come and shake us, but with the Son's help and with friends to hold us up, the storm will pass, and soon the sun will shine again. These storms help us stand taller and be stronger than before.

REFLECTION:

What do you need to do to help your seed grow?
How deep are your roots?

> *"And which of you by being anxious can add a single hour to his span*
> *of life? And why are you anxious about clothing? Consider the lilies*
> *of the field, how they grow: they neither toil nor spin, yet I tell you,*
> *even Solomon in all his glory was not arrayed like one of these."*
> ~ Matthew 6:27-29 (ESV)

5

Rough Waters

I recently enjoyed a long weekend at a cottage on Lake Ontario. My spirit is always renewed being near bodies of water, just gazing at the beauty of the world God created. An added bonus is that this area is the perfect spot to view God's sunset masterpieces.

I thoroughly enjoyed the contrasts Lake Ontario held with the water. The first and last day there, it felt like I was at the ocean. The first day, it was chilly and windy, which made the water rough and wavy. The waves were crashing along the shoreline. The other days, the water was calm and quiet, with no waves. I was mesmerized seeing how the wind's effect made the water flow in different directions on different days.

I began to think about the parallels between water, waves, wind, and God in our lives.

No matter if our lives are stormy, tumultuous, or calm,
>> no matter what way the wind is blowing,
>>> the one constant is God,
>>>> the anchor to keep us grounded.

What can we learn from Bible verses referencing rough waters?

"I hear the tumult of the raging seas as your waves and surging tides sweep over me. But each day the Lord pours his unfailing love upon me, and through each night I sing his songs, praying to God who gives me life."
~ Psalm 42:7-8 (NLT)

Christine M. Fisher

What a dismal picture the psalmist paints with his description of the raging seas and tides overtaking him. Water often symbolizes chaos and confusion in Scripture. The second part of the psalm gives us great encouragement. God pours out His unfailing love in the storms of life, so much so that we are able to sing praises of thanksgiving to the Lord.

"I am the Lord your God, who stirs up the sea so that its waves roar—the Lord of hosts is his name. And I have put my words in your mouth and covered you in the shadow of my hand, establishing the heavens and laying the foundations of the earth, and saying to Zion, 'You are my people.'"
~ Isaiah 51:15-16 (ESV)

God reigns over the seas, making the waves appear symbolic of the storms in our lives. Our God is so great that He cares for you and me as He gives us the words to speak life into our storms. God also protects us in the shadow of His hand, not letting us ever be alone. We are His precious creation whom He cares for.

"The seas have lifted up, Lord, the seas have lifted up their voice; the seas have lifted up their pounding waves. Mightier than the thunder of the great waters, mightier than the breakers of the sea—the Lord on high is mighty."
~ Psalm 93:3-4

Being on the sea during a mighty storm, we can experience great turbulence and noise as the waves pound against the boat. The Lord is even mightier in power than the waves of the open sea. God's Word is more thunderous and powerful than the stormiest of seas.

Just as boats are equipped with anchors that attach to the bottom of the sea, providing stability to help steady the boat and stop it from drifting, we have an anchor during the storms of life. As Christians, Jesus is our anchor to help us weather the storms.

"So God has given both his promise and his oath. These two things are unchangeable because it is impossible for God to lie. Therefore, we who have fled to him for refuge can have great confidence as we hold to the hope that lies before us. This hope is a strong and trustworthy anchor for our souls. It leads us through the curtain into God's inner sanctuary. Jesus has already gone in there for us. He has become our eternal High Priest in the order of Melchizedek."
~ Hebrews 6:18-20 (NLT)

Jesus is our anchor and hope to steady us during the rough waters of this life. His hope and love help us be immovable as the tides come crashing upon us. We can trust Jesus and remain strong in Him.

In the rough waters and the storms of life, be encouraged to…

> see God's unfailing love giving life and victory.
> speak life over the storms.
> seek protection in the shadow of God's hand.
> turn to God's Word, which is mightier than the stormy seas.
> remain attached to the anchor for our soul, Jesus.

No matter if our lives are stormy, tumultuous, or calm,
   no matter what way the wind is blowing,
      the one constant is God,
         the anchor to keep us grounded.

REFLECTION:

What rough waters has Jesus gotten you through by being your anchor? Do you have comfort knowing you can trust Jesus?

> *"The voice of the Lord is over the waters; the God of glory thunders, the Lord thunders over the mighty waters."*
> ~ Psalm 29:3

Christine M. Fisher

6

Silence is Golden

What great truth there is in the saying:

Silence is golden.

At a retreat I attended, silence was one of the first things that was introduced and then implemented for the rest of the evening.

As the leader pointed out,

Silence is actually a gift you give yourself and others.

Have you ever viewed silence as a gift?

Especially in today's technological world, how many times do you see someone **not** tied to their phone? People are either texting, listening to music or a podcast with headphones, or talking on their phone. No matter if we are riding on a bus, walking somewhere, or even at a restaurant, most likely we are engaged with our phones. With our fast-paced lives, how much room do you leave for silence?

We were encouraged at this retreat to spend time in silence. Though it was dark, I couldn't wait to get outside. Knowing the lake was in the distance, I just wanted to walk around, God and me. The quietness I experienced was beautiful. When I first went outside, I observed the pure silence that surrounded me. After a few minutes, there was a single noise from some kind of creature, and a few minutes later, one from the opposite side.

Then suddenly, there was pure silence in the dark of the night. It truly was golden, and I could sense the oneness of the silence between God and me. I wanted to keep soaking it up, every pore of my being immersed in silence, in Him. I walked around and then stood with my eyes shut, in solitude with my Creator. What a wonderful gift.

Silence and experiencing silence are ways to connect with God.

> Silence, just being present, and not thinking about the many things you need to get done.

>> Silence and taking time to be alone with God in solitude and not attached to some electronic device.

>>> Silence with the Lord in the sense of not telling Him what we think His plan for you, or your loved ones, should be.

Silence is a type of prayer.

> Silence ushers us into God's presence.

>> Silence fills us with even more of His love and peace.

If you don't currently take time to be silent, I challenge you to take five minutes one day and leave your phone or electronic devices in the other room. Find a place where you can be alone—some room in your house, outside, or at a church—and experience God in the silence. Just **be**.

If you do take time to be silent, I encourage you to keep it up. Give yourself the gift of silence and experience God's presence.

Silence is golden.

REFLECTION:

How often do you take time to experience silence?
Where is your favorite place to go and be silent?

"Then Moses said to Aaron, 'This is what the Lord meant when he said, "I will display my holiness through those who come near me. I will display my glory before all the people."' And Aaron was silent."
~ Leviticus 10:3 (NLT)

7

Faith and Trust

Fall time in the northeast USA is always a breath-taking blessing to experience. I find it a beautiful season where we can see God's hand working to make such a beautiful masterpiece, which we get to behold with our eyes. The green leaves on the trees start to turn different hues of yellow, orange, and red. It is quite a sight to see. For those who have never experienced the fall colors, I do hope someday you will be able to. Seeing the rolling hills and mountains, especially in the beautiful fall array of colors that God provides, brings me into a closer relationship with the Creator and His glory.

I recently had the privilege of going on a short-day trip in the fall, and as is typical, I felt enveloped in the Lord's presence. It was as if His majestic power and beauty were all around me as I looked upon the Grand Canyon of Pennsylvania in Wellsboro.

There are different stopping points to view nature. It was quite a trek to go from one scenic part to another. For me, it was a trek that exercised my faith and trust in God. I thought about that, especially since I was alone at the time and, because there was no cell service, there was no way to contact anyone if I ran into trouble.

What if I had a flat tire?

What if the car broke down?

What if something happened?

I tried to put those thoughts out of my head and trust the Lord like we must continually do every day. Listening to some Mac Powell country music also seemed fitting to help me relax.

Things didn't get off to a great start. As I was leaving stop one, the GPS told me to turn on what looked like a narrow dirt road. Obediently, I turned onto the road and, after driving a short distance, a closed gate was my clue that I was driving down a walking path. I didn't have space to turn around, so I put the car in reverse and slowly backed down.

Getting to stop two took faith and trust in God, and the GPS, which I'm never quite sure of. I find it strange that one day the GPS can lead one way, and another day it will take a different path. My husband always says it is a very complicated algorithm and wonders if I'm up to perfecting it.

At one point, I crossed over a paved road and onto a dirt road that had an incline and seemed wide enough for only one car. I prayed that a car wouldn't be coming the other way. At first, I doubted the GPS, but I figured at least the time was counting down to my arrival time, so I had no choice but to trust it. Sure enough, I made it safely to stop two.

It was a gorgeous view, though the trees were mostly green and yellow, not so colorful on this particular day. It was where I felt God's majesty envelope me—the huge, massive hills—and what looked like a giant heart carved in the scenery that only the Creator could do.

I decided to walk one of the trails despite, once again, the *what if* thoughts running through my head. I'm not really the mountain-climber type, and I was all alone.

What if I fell?
> What if I got lost?
> > What if…?

But, again, I tried to put those thoughts out of my head and decided to trust and have faith.

The view was awesome from the one outlook spot, so I was thankful I ventured down the path. The view of the water was closer, and I am always blessed to reflect on the beauty of the water.

Stop three was a fifty minute ride; once again with intense curves, narrow roads, some one-lane bridges where I prayed no one was coming, and roads that required me to step out in faith. The drive was beautiful because, at points, I was close to the water and the sides of the huge mountains. It was like I was right at the base and could see how massive and majestic they were. The hills were covered with a beautiful array of yellow trees.

Once there, I found a perfect spot next to the water, sat in my chair, and started to pen my adventure. In typical fashion, I began to soak up the Son's presence, listening to the wind blowing and the birds' echoing squawks.

I knew I was in the Lord's presence when I looked up in the sky. What first caught my eye were three clouds, the only ones gracing the clear blue sky. Right among those three clouds was a lone bird, quickly joined by a second bird, and then a third. It reminded me of God the Father, Jesus, His Son, and the Holy Spirit. Three in one in me.

God is a mighty God, and He makes His presence known in the beauty of nature. Take a moment and enjoy His presence and glory today.

"Where can I go from your Spirit? Where can I flee from your presence? If I go up to the heavens, you are there; if I make my bed in the depths, you are there. If I rise on the wings of the dawn, if I settle on the far side of the sea, even there your hand will guide me, your right hand will hold me fast."
~ Psalm 139:7-10

Christine M. Fisher

Continue to trust God to help you through your struggles and have faith that His presence, the Holy Spirit, is with you always.

REFLECTION:

In what situation have you had to place all your faith and trust in God to make it through?
What nature scene did you experience God's glory in?

"Glorify the Lord with me; let us exalt his name together. I sought the Lord, and he answered me; he delivered me from all my fears."
~ Psalm 34:3-4

8

Slow Down

In this fast-paced and technologically advanced world we live in, it is important to slow down and see God's glory in our lives and in the world around us.

When we are continually running and doing things, we can miss out on God all around us.

Slow down and take time to see God's glory…

feeling the gentle wind sweep across your body.
viewing the clouds and cloud formations God put in the sky for you to behold.
being amazed at how the trees rebirth every year.
considering the wildflowers that grace the fields.
soaking up His Spirit in the warmth of the sun beating down on you.
watching the graceful birds that soar in the sky, singing God's praises.
marveling at the amazing creatures that roam around, like deer, rabbits, and chipmunks.

It is most important to slow down and take time to see God's glory…

in each person God places in our path, from the stranger you hold the door open for to your best friend.

Christine M. Fisher

We are all made in God's image; that makes each person a treasure. He loves each of us with everlasting love.

Getting to know your neighbor will help you...

> understand why they are like they are.
> see where they've been.
> realize the joys and sorrows they've endured.
> treat all with respect.
> better serve everyone you meet.

By doing these things, your life will be enriched even more.

Slow down and take time to see God's glory in...

> the silence.
> the peace and solitude.
> tranquil times.

May the busyness of life not distract you too much. Slow down and take time to see God's glory everywhere—in all of nature, every person you encounter, and even in the silence.

REFLECTION:

How have you experienced God's glory in nature?
Is there a neighbor you need to take time to get to know better?

> *"Praise be to the Lord God, the God of Israel, who alone does marvelous deeds. Praise be to his glorious name forever; may the whole earth be filled with his glory. Amen and Amen."*
> ~ Psalm 72:18-19

9

Step by Step

One summer, while on vacation with my family, I conquered something that was difficult for me. On a much smaller scale, I also did a similar activity recently. This activity produces sweaty hands and fear within me, and my mind doubts that all will be okay.

I am still afraid of heights!

My earliest recollection of this fear was as a young child. Sitting high up in the arena, I recall feeling or thinking that I could fall straight down. What if gravity stopped working? I would surely tumble down all the seats and land at the bottom of the arena. I know that would be the first time gravity ever stopped working, but somehow that did not stop fear from creeping in.

Back to the summer vacation: the thought of doing seven ziplines, back to back, on a family excursion was fine until we approached the zipline. I was relieved it was the first of three activities we were going to do, knowing I could relax afterward. That is, if I survived. As a side note, the ATV drive that followed the ziplines was worse than the ziplines. The ride turned out to be so rough that I was thrown around while trying to hold on for dear life.

As I approached the first zipline stair area, I could hear a little girl screaming; she eventually made her way back down the stairs. That was not the best scene for me, but I figured I did not want to be like that girl, so the challenge was on. I wanted to conquer the seven ziplines. It was reassuring to know that I could choose to do just three or five of the lines if I wanted to stop early.

Since the other families in our group went first, I decided to be the last one to go within our family. In the beginning, I would wait at the bottom of the first set of stairs until everyone else above me was out of the way. Then I would start up the next level. That way, I could keep going, as bravely as I could, one step at a time, and not get stuck on a stair. These stairs were made of what appeared to be tree wood, sometimes a little uneven, and there was fencing around them. Though I knew it was safe, fear ensued. My hands became sweaty as I placed them on the two railings to begin my ascent.

All I could think of was, "take one step at a time and keep going." And that's what I did.

Once I made it to the first zipline, it was an amazing feeling to zip through the air amidst the many jungle-type trees below. It was fun, which inspired me to keep going.

I had not considered that, since there were seven stations, every station meant more and more steps. More and more steps meant we were technically getting higher and higher from the safety of the ground. Yikes!

What also gave me courage was that, in the first few ziplines, there was no waiting once we got to the top of the platform. That way, I could just keep moving and not dwell on how high I was. As soon as we reached the platform, the helpers would hook us to a safety line, so there was no chance of falling or slipping.

At the fourth station, there was an option to zipline as Superman on your stomach or upside down. I forced myself to do the Superman style! Yes, I did.

The hardest part was getting parallel to the ground to get harnessed in. (My hands are a little sweaty as I type these thoughts.) I held one of the helper's hands as I was shaking. The Superman style was fun, but only my youngest son was brave enough to try the upside down option.

Fast forward to more recently. While visiting my daughter at college, my husband and I explored a nearby lighthouse. We took a tour of the keeper's house and climbed 55 stairs to the top of the lighthouse. As we ascended the spiral staircase, my hands started sweating, and fear quickly crept in. The last few stairs at the top did not have a railing, so that made it harder. The fear continued as I looked out at the top, so I kept holding on to the railing as I walked slowly around to catch the different views. Our tour guide was kind and understood my agony. He said he literally crawled on his hands and knees the first time he climbed those last few stairs.

Why am I sharing these thoughts? Because when I was climbing those stairs at the ziplines and repeating to myself, "one step at a time," I thought it was a good reminder of our daily walk with the Lord.

Isn't it all too easy to let fear overtake us, even in our daily circumstances?

Do you ever find yourself wondering what the future holds?

Things like…

> How will our children turn out?
> What will happen if we become disabled?
> Will we have enough money to survive?
> What happens if that cancer recurs?

May I encourage you when fear starts to creep in…

> it's okay to do something you're afraid of doing.
> to let your faith be greater than your fear.

Christine M. Fisher

to focus on taking one step at a time.

to look straight ahead, keeping your eyes on the Lord.

to give glory to God for helping you overcome.

And remind yourself that…

your faith in God is greater than your fear.

God is a mighty God.

He is victorious and a conqueror.

step by step, God will lead and provide.

REFLECTION:

What has God gotten you through where you took one step at a time?
What fear have you conquered with God's help?

*"For I, the Lord your God, hold your right hand; it is I who say to you,
'Fear not, I am the one who helps you. Fear not, you worm Jacob, you men
of Israel! I am the one who helps you,' declares the Lord; your Redeemer
is the Holy One of Israel. 'Behold, I make of you a threshing sledge, new,
sharp, and having teeth; you shall thresh the mountains and crush them,
and you shall make the hills like chaff; you shall winnow them, and the
wind shall carry them away, and the tempest shall scatter them. And you
shall rejoice in the Lord; in the Holy One of Israel you shall glory.'"*
~ Isaiah 41:13-16 (ESV)

10

Little Day Brighteners

This Facebook post from a friend is an excellent reminder for us.

"Sometimes we forget about all the little things we could do to brighten someone's day—to show love to others without expecting anything in return. I was the receiver of these beautiful flowers from a dear friend yesterday!"

Didn't Jesus tell us the importance of the little things in life—sharing God's love with everyone without expecting anything in return?

"Are not two sparrows sold for a penny? Yet not one of them will fall to the ground outside your Father's care. And even the very hairs of your head are all numbered. So don't be afraid; you are worth more than many sparrows."
~ Matthew 10:29-31

Jesus teaches us how God cares for the littlest of creation, the sparrows. They are not worth much in this world, but God loves them because He created them. The number of hairs on our head is hardly worthy of our attention, but Jesus uses the example to show us how much God cares for us. We are all valuable in God's kingdom.

Can you think of a time when someone did something little that made your day much brighter?

Did someone…

> bring you flowers to show that you are loved?
> send you an encouraging text?

Christine M. Fisher

sincerely wish you a special day?

bring you coffee or a treat?

invite you to dine with them?

who was a stranger talk to you when you felt all alone?

How did something little make you feel?

Maybe…

loved?

joyful?

special?

important?

valued?

My daughter surprised me recently by leaving a little treasure on my porch. I did not find it randomly, like she was hoping, because her joy couldn't be contained. Nonetheless, I could not help but beam from ear to ear thinking of her planning this surprise, which is out of character for her.

I recall one day I was sharing with a friend what their reflection meant to me personally. The friend picked up on something and sent me a few encouraging prayers. It was something small, yet, it had a profound impact that breathed life into my spirit.

Can you think of times when you reached out to do something little for someone else to brighten their day and share love, not expecting anything in return?

Was it something from the list above or something else?

Isn't it fun to do little things to brighten someone's day?

We never know when the smallest of things will become the greatest blessing in another person's life.

I have often found the ripple effect of God's goodness when I step out to do something little for someone. One time, I went out of my way to deliver something special—a surprise—to a friend. When I was driving home, I saw a CVS tractor trailer that had a big red heart in the middle of the cab. This made me smile, as I knew God's perfect timing and goodness was letting me know He saw me sharing His love.

Often, I see the ripple effect of sending a text to someone as a reminder of God's love, and mine, or sending a word of encouragement. This often leads to more of His orchestrations. In one case, it led the person to share they were feeling down as there was a remembrance service that day for their loved one. It inspired me to attend the service to show my support for their family, though I had never met the one they lost. After lighting a candle in their loved one's memory, the person stopped to thank me and took my hand in gratitude. I felt the Spirit's presence in that encounter, knowing it was another God moment. My friend later shared, "Seeing your face and holding your hand was beautiful and comforting."

Life is made up of little moments—little moments that we can use to brighten other people's days and to show God's love—without expecting anything in return.

Be encouraged to…

> share little things to brighten other people's days.
> appreciate the little things others do to brighten your day.
> show God's love without expecting anything in return.

Take the little you have and let God do something great with it.

REFLECTION:

What is something someone did to brighten your day?
How did you bless someone and make their day a little brighter?

> *"So whether you eat or drink or whatever you*
> *do, do it all for the glory of God."*
> ~ 1 Corinthians 10:31

11

Water Reminders

Since I was a young girl, I remember experiencing a closeness to God while spending time at the seashore. I am still in awe of being near bodies of water, whether it be the ocean, a lake, or a river. It never grows old; rather, it is life-giving and refreshing for my spirit.

It has been a nice exercise to reflect on why I enjoy water so much while searching Scripture. What makes God's creation of water areas so special to me?

The water reminds me of God.

THE WATER REMINDS ME THAT I HAVE ONENESS WITH GOD.

> *"In the beginning God created the heavens and the earth. Now the earth was formless and empty, darkness was over the surface of the deep, and the Spirit of God was hovering over the waters."*
> ~ Genesis 1:1-2

We know God has always existed. He formed the heavens and the earth. The earth was totally empty, yet water was present with God in the beginning. God's Spirit was hovering over the waters. Maybe that is why I feel oneness with God when I'm near the water. I long to experience the Spirit of God in my life and oneness with Him.

THE WATER REMINDS ME THAT GOD IS WITH ME DURING THE RAGING WATERS OF LIFE.

Christine M. Fisher

"When you pass through the waters, I will be with you; and when you pass through the rivers, they will not sweep over you..."
~ Isaiah 43:2

When I am at the ocean, watching the waves roaring in as they crash into the shore and then dissipate, I am reminded that God is with me through the raging storms. He will not let me be swept away in the rough waters. What a comfort that is.

THE WATER REMINDS ME OF THE JOY WE HAVE IN KNOWING GOD AS OUR ABBA.

"Behold, God is my salvation; I will trust, and will not be afraid; for the Lord God is my strength and my song, and he has become my salvation. With joy you will draw water from the wells of salvation. And you will say in that day: Give thanks to the Lord, call upon his name, make known his deeds among the peoples, proclaim that his name is exalted."
~ Isaiah 12:2-4 (ESV)

We have the gift of salvation because of God and Jesus. Daily, we grow in trust and fear less because we know God is our strength. The water symbolizes the joy we have in knowing the Lord, giving thanks to Him, and sharing His glorious deeds and name with others.

THE WATER REMINDS ME THAT THE LORD WILL GUIDE ME CONTINUALLY.

"And the Lord will guide you continually and satisfy your desire in scorched places and make your bones strong; and you shall be like a watered garden, like a spring of water, whose waters do not fail."
~ Isaiah 58:11 (ESV)

The vastness of the ocean reminds me that God is always guiding us. No matter what the circumstances of our lives, He is guiding us and making us stronger in Him. We have His assurance that our water source will never dry up.

THE WATER REMINDS ME THAT GOD PROVIDES PEACE AND TRANQUILITY IN OUR LIVES.

> *"He makes me lie down in green pastures, he leads me*
> *beside quiet waters, he refreshes my soul…"*
> ~ Psalm 23:2-3

When the waters are calm, I am filled with peace and tranquility, knowing deep in my spirit that life is okay no matter what is happening. God is at the center of my life, and in my heart, so I can experience the peace that surpasses all understanding.

The water reminds me of Jesus.

THE WATER REMINDS ME OF WHEN JESUS WAS BAPTIZED.

> *"One day Jesus came from Nazareth in Galilee, and John*
> *baptized him in the Jordan River. As Jesus came up out of the*
> *water, he saw the heavens splitting apart and the Holy Spirit*
> *descending on him like a dove. And a voice from heaven said,*
> *'You are my dearly loved Son, and you bring me great joy.'"*
> ~ Mark 1:9-11 (NLT)

I am grateful for the opportunity I had to visit the Jordan River, where Jesus was baptized. Water is symbolic of the new life we are granted when we are baptized. We become God's dearly loved son or daughter, just as Jesus did.

THE WATER REMINDS ME HOW JESUS' COMMAND CAN CALM STORMS IN OUR LIVES.

Christine M. Fisher

"One day Jesus said to his disciples, 'Let us go over to the other side of the lake.' So they got into a boat and set out. As they sailed, he fell asleep. A squall came down on the lake, so that the boat was being swamped, and they were in great danger. The disciples went and woke him, saying, 'Master, Master, we're going to drown!' He got up and rebuked the wind and the raging waters; the storm subsided, and all was calm. 'Where is your faith?' he asked his disciples. In fear and amazement, they asked one another, 'Who is this? He commands even the winds and the water, and they obey him.'"
~ Luke 8:22-25

This story shows Jesus' power over the storms in our lives. Jesus, in His humanity, fell asleep shortly after getting into the boat. He trusted that everything would work out because He knew that, ultimately, God is in control. When the disciples woke Jesus in their panic, He got up and rebuked the wind and waters, so the lake was calm. The disciples were shocked when they saw what Jesus did. Jesus wanted them to have faith, just as He wants us to have faith during the storms in our lives.

THE WATER REMINDS ME HOW I ALWAYS WANT THE LIVING WATERS FLOWING FROM MY HEART.

"On the last day of the feast, the great day, Jesus stood up and cried out, 'If anyone thirsts, let him come to me and drink. Whoever believes in me, as the Scripture has said, "Out of his heart will flow rivers of living water."'"
~ John 7:37-38 (ESV)

I never want to be thirsty again, but if I am, I know to fill up with Jesus. When we believe in Jesus, we are assured that, from our hearts, rivers of His living water will flow into the lives of all we encounter. What a great blessing to be assured of. The living water in us will spill over into others' lives and impact them.

May rivers of living water flow from us.

May you be encouraged, even if you're not near bodies of water, of…

> being one with God.
> God being with you in the raging waters of life.
> the joy of knowing God is your Abba.
> the Lord guiding you.
> God providing peace and tranquility for you.
> Jesus' baptism.
> Jesus commanding the calming of storms.
> the living waters flowing from your heart.

Spirit of God, hover over each of our lives, just as You did over the waters before You formed heaven and earth. Wash over us, changing us to be more like You. In the ebb and flow of life, help us hold onto You, knowing You calm the storms in our lives and provide peace. Quench our thirst and let our hearts flow with Your living water. We ask all this in Jesus' precious name. Amen.

REFLECTION:

Which water reminder above speaks to your spirit the most?
What storm has Jesus calmed in your life?

> *"For as the waters fill the sea, the earth will be filled*
> *with an awareness of the glory of the Lord."*
> ~ Habakkuk 2:14 (NLT)

Christine M. Fisher

12

Great Love

Over the past few years, God has impressed most upon my spirit the theme of **love**. I experience love from above when I see the almost daily heart reminders in whatever physical form they take.

A friend was excited to share this picture and message she received. It reminds me of the great love Jesus has for us and the importance of sharing His love with others. A simple gesture can brighten someone's day, knowing they are loved from above and by others.

A few Scriptures about God's love for us:

"But God showed his great love for us by sending Christ to die for us while we were still sinners. And since we have been made right in God's sight by the blood of Christ, he will certainly save us from God's condemnation."
~ Romans 5:8-9 (NLT)

"God showed how much he loved us by sending his one and only Son into the world so that we might have eternal life through him. This is real love—not that we loved God, but that he loved us and sent his Son as a sacrifice to take away our sins."
~ 1 John 4:9-10 (NLT)

God's love for us, His beloved children, is so great that, after Adam and Eve sinned by disobeying God and eating from the tree of knowledge, He laid out the plan to restore our relationship. In His great love, God had Jesus, His only begotten Son, leave Him for a time and walk on this earth. His plan for salvation was for Jesus to die on the cross, shedding His blood, to set you and me free. Jesus' brutal death grants us salvation to spend eternity in heaven.

Is the depth of your heart filled with gratitude for God's great love in sending Jesus, His only Son, to restore your relationship with Him?

A few Scriptures about Jesus' love for us:

"As the Father has loved me, so have I loved you. Now remain in my love."
~ John 15:9

"There is no greater love than to lay down one's life for one's friends."
~ John 15:13 (NLT)

Can you fathom the love Jesus had for God, His Father? Jesus' love for God was so great that He obediently died on the cross, so all who believe can be one with God. Jesus endured agony as He was whipped, beaten, and hung on a cross because He loved us with that same great love. That makes me feel special. Jesus shared that there is no greater love than dying for someone else.

Do you personally experience the depth of Jesus' love and willingness to die on the cross for you?

A few Scriptures about our responsibility to love:

"Dear friends, let us love one another, for love comes from God. Everyone who loves has been born of God and knows God. Whoever does not love does not know God, because God is love."
~ 1 John 4:7-8

"A new command I give you: Love one another. As I have loved you, so you must love one another. By this everyone will know that you are my disciples, if you love one another."
~ John 13:34-35

As we realize the vastness of the great love God and Jesus have for us, we are called to share that same love with all we encounter. God is love, and He is the source of love. If we believe in God, we must also love. Because Jesus shared His love of the Father with us, He commands that we, too, love one another. The greatest attribute of a disciple of Jesus is love.

Do you love others with the intensity of love you have received from God and Jesus?

God is love, and He created us in love and made us in His image. What love God, the Father, bestowed upon us, letting us be called children of God. While Jesus walked on this earth, He loved the least of us and went about healing those in need. We are commanded to love others, even our enemies, because of the love God and Jesus have shown us. We have been loved much, so we need to love much.

Be encouraged to reflect on...

> knowing that God loved you first.
> knowing that Jesus loves you as much as He loves God.
> loving others with the same love that Jesus has for you.

And remember, Jesus loves you, and so do I.

REFLECTION:

When is the first time you realized the depth of God's love for you? How did you step out in faith to love a stranger like Jesus does?

> *"Not to us, O Lord, not to us, but to your name goes all*
> *the glory for your unfailing love and faithfulness."*
> ~ Psalm 115:1 (NLT)

13

Holy Ground

Holy ground…

What thoughts come to mind when reading those words?
Have you been somewhere that you consider holy ground?
Or, has some encounter been holy ground for you?

My definition of holy ground would be somewhere sacred, peaceful, serene, and tranquil where I experience a oneness with the Lord, seeing and feeling His presence.

I have experienced holy ground…

in sunrises and sunsets.
in the beauty of bodies of water, like the ocean.
at some worship services.
at Christian concerts.
in the presence and stillness of someone near death.
in certain times of prayer.
in the majestic mountains.
in my car listening to inspiring music.

There are two main ways I experience holy ground in my life.

Sometimes it is the environment or physical surroundings that make something holy ground for me. One such physical place is where I attended a retreat several years ago. At the back of the retreat house, my eyes could behold beautiful Canandaigua Lake with rolling hills in the background.

Looking at the rolling hills and the water, along with the sun beaming down from the sky, makes it holy ground for me. On my last visit, a gal mentioned an isolated pond on the side of the property, so I enjoyed walking there while observing some deer strolling along, listening to the birds singing. I was glad I did not see the fox she mentioned.

Sometimes it is the quiet, peaceful encounter in prayer or worship that marks holy ground for me. Examples are some church services, times at Third Day concerts (my favorite Christian band), and sometimes listening to inspiring Christian music in my car.

> *"Now Moses was tending the flock of Jethro his father-in-law, the priest of Midian, and he led the flock to the far side of the wilderness and came to Horeb, the mountain of God. There the angel of the Lord appeared to him in flames of fire from within a bush. Moses saw that though the bush was on fire it did not burn up. So Moses thought, 'I will go over and see this strange sight— why the bush does not burn up.' When the Lord saw that he had gone over to look, God called to him from within the bush, 'Moses! Moses!' And Moses said, 'Here I am.' 'Do not come any closer,' God said. 'Take off your sandals, for the place where you are standing is holy ground.' Then he said, 'I am the God of your father, the God of Abraham, the God of Isaac and the God of Jacob.' At this, Moses hid his face, because he was afraid to look at God.*

> *"The Lord said, 'I have indeed seen the misery of my people in Egypt. I have heard them crying out because of their slave drivers, and I am concerned about their suffering. So I have come down to rescue them from the hand of the Egyptians and to bring them up out of that land into a good and spacious land, a land flowing with milk and honey—the home of the Canaanites, Hittites, Amorites, Perizzites, Hivites and Jebusites. And now the cry of the Israelites has reached me, and I have seen the way*

the Egyptians are oppressing them. So now, go. I am sending you
to Pharaoh to bring my people the Israelites out of Egypt.'''
~ Exodus 3:1-10

While Moses was tending sheep in the wilderness, an angel of the Lord appeared to him in the flames of fire from a burning bush. He was trying to find out why the bush was not burning up despite the flames. In the burning bush, God spoke to Moses, saying he was standing on holy ground and to take his sandals off. What a special moment for Moses. God had concern for the suffering of the Egyptians and assured Moses they would reach the Promised Land. God is compassionate.

REFLECTION:

Where have you experienced holy ground?
What is your most memorable instance of holy ground?

"To the Israelites the glory of the Lord looked like a consuming fire on
top of the mountain. Then Moses entered the cloud as he went on up the
mountain. And he stayed on the mountain forty days and forty nights."
~ Exodus 24:17-18

Christine M. Fisher

14

The Cedar Tree

I received a special treasure, a masterpiece from nature. This gift is from a cedar tree that was on my friend's property. He knew I would appreciate adding it to my heart collection, which reminds me of the importance of love in our lives. The outside is heart-shaped, and there is a heart-shape on the inside.

Notice the unique wood grain color present at the bottom, right in the heart.

It is amazing to see the transformation that took place when it was sanded and then covered in clear enamel, which brings out the intricacies of the wood grain as well as the brightness of the heart. How did God make this cedar tree have a natural red heart in it?

As I look in wonder at this treasure, I reflect on what God might be revealing to us about trees.

"Now the Lord God had planted a garden in the east, in Eden; and there he put the man he had formed. The Lord God made all kinds of trees grow out of the ground—trees that were pleasing to the eye and good for food. In the middle of the garden were the tree of life and the tree of the knowledge of good and evil."
~ Genesis 2:8-9

From the beginning, God put Adam, the first man He breathed life into, in the middle of a beautiful garden, which consisted of different kinds of trees. The man was in awe of the beauty of the trees, which provided nourishment for him.

"Praise the Lord from the earth, you great sea creatures and all ocean depths, lightning and hail, snow and clouds, stormy winds that do his bidding, you mountains and all hills, fruit trees and all cedars, wild animals and all cattle, small creatures and flying birds, kings of the earth and all nations, you princes and all rulers on earth, young men and women, old men and children. Let them praise the name of the Lord, for his name alone is exalted; his splendor is above the earth and the heavens."
~ Psalm 148:7-13

God made all creation—from the sea creatures to the weather, to the animals, to the people—to praise the Lord, the Creator. We all have our unique ways of praising. I believe this heart treasure gives praise to the Lord by displaying and reminding us of His beauty and love, which we can behold when gazing upon it.

I was curious to see what Scripture references there were to cedar trees, as well as wanting to learn about cedar trees.

Biblically, cedar trees are known for being...

Christine M. Fisher

PLANTED BY GOD.

*"The trees of the Lord are watered abundantly, the cedars
of Lebanon that he planted. In them the birds build their
nests; the stork has her home in the fir trees."*
~ Psalm 104:16-17 (ESV)

A MODEL FOR THE RIGHTEOUS.

*"The righteous flourish like the palm tree and grow like
a cedar in Lebanon. They are planted in the house of the
Lord; they flourish in the courts of our God."*
~ Psalm 92:12-13 (ESV)

STRONG AND DURABLE.

*"The bricks have fallen down, but we will rebuild with dressed stone;
the fig trees have been felled, but we will replace them with cedars."*
~ Isaiah 9:10

TALL AND NOBLE.

*"This is what the Sovereign Lord says: I will take a
branch from the top of a tall cedar, and I will plant
it on the top of Israel's highest mountain."*
~ Ezekiel 17:22 (NLT)

GOOD SHADE.

*"It will become a majestic cedar, sending forth its branches
and producing seed. Birds of every sort will nest in it,
finding shelter in the shade of its branches."*
~ Ezekiel 17:23 (NLT)

"Your lips are as sweet as nectar, my bride. Honey and milk are under your tongue. Your clothes are scented like the cedars of Lebanon."
~ Song of Songs 4:11 (NLT)

The back of this heart is also interesting. Notice that the darker color is not a heart shape on the back side.

Can you see the small teacup shape with the dark rim facing upward and the steam coming out of the top? It reminds me of Jesus sharing the cup of wine with His disciples at the Last Supper.

"And he took a cup of wine and gave thanks to God for it. He gave it to them and said, 'Each of you drink from it, for this is my blood, which confirms the covenant between God and his people. It is poured out as a sacrifice to forgive the sins of many.'"
~ Matthew 26:27-28 (NLT)

Both the front and back of this treasure have the lighter colored rectangle inside the wood grain. I think it may have symbolism because it is placed inside the heart. At first glance, it almost looks like a band-aid, which could symbolize the hole in our hearts that only Jesus can fill. Our hearts are restless until they rest in the Lord. Or it could represent when Jesus died, and His side was pierced.

> *"But when they came to Jesus and found that he was already dead, they did not break his legs. Instead, one of the soldiers pierced Jesus' side with a spear, bringing a sudden flow of blood and water. The man who saw it has given testimony, and his testimony is true. He knows that he tells the truth, and he testifies so that you also may believe."*
> ~ John 19:33-35

When the soldier pierced Jesus' side, the flow of blood and water appeared as a result of the spear piercing the sac around Jesus' heart and the heart itself. It can be a reminder of that piercing and the great love that Jesus has for each one of us in giving His life to set us free. When I look at this cedar heart treasure, it reminds me of Jesus' burning love for all humanity to come to Him.

May you be reminded of the cedar tree and remember to…

be in awe of the beauty of the trees.
look for ways all of God's creation praises Him.
seek ways your life can flourish for the Lord.

be strong in the Lord and in your faith.
stand firmly planted in the Lord.
sow good seeds of righteousness.

waft the aroma—the fragrance of God.
appreciate Jesus' sacrifice of His blood for your salvation.
thank Jesus for His burning love for all of humanity.

REFLECTION:

Has God revealed to you a masterpiece in nature that reflects His love?
Which attribute of the cedar tree do you need to model more?

> *"The desert and the parched land will be glad; the wilderness*
> *will rejoice and blossom. Like the crocus, it will burst into bloom;*
> *it will rejoice greatly and shout for joy. The glory of Lebanon*
> *will be given to it, the splendor of Carmel and Sharon; they*
> *will see the glory of the Lord, the splendor of our God."*
> ~ Isaiah 35:1-2

15

Everyday Miracles

Do you ever stop and wonder why we don't see great miracles like in Jesus' day? Maybe we need to reflect on our current lifestyles and the little miracles that occur every day in order to gain a better perspective on this question.

Our lifestyles are rather instant and technically advanced, compared to Jesus' day. We rush and run from one place to another, merely doing our routine. All this advancement is great, as long as we keep the proper perspective on life.

Amidst the hustle and bustle of each day, we need to take time to see the little miracles God sends our way.

The miracle of nature with…

> the sun and moon that appear each day.
> the seasons that come year after year.
> the birds that fly south to keep warm.
> the trees that change with the seasons.

The miracle of your body with…

> how you were formed in your mother's womb.
> your ears, which can hear all kinds of sounds.
> the blood pumping through your body that performs so many functions.
> your eyes that allow you to see beautiful sights.

The miracle of circumstances in your life with…

the relationship that was restored.

the people who offered to pray for you, helping you through a health crisis.

how you found strength to make it through a long, rough patch at work.

how you overcame an addiction.

A co-worker told me about how another co-worker was on his way to his car when someone stopped and asked for help. This interruption occurred at just the perfect time. Had he not stopped to help, he would have been getting into his car at the same time the ramp collapsed where his car was parked. Thank you, Lord, for that everyday miracle.

I was at a minor baseball league game with my youngest son when I ran into a co-worker. As we hugged each other, I noticed a cross necklace she was wearing. The next day at work, I felt led to share my website with her, and we talked about God and my favorite band, Third Day. She said this was just what she needed to help her through a rough time. I consider that baseball game encounter and our follow-up discussion an everyday miracle.

I also consider the orchestration of my website, hopetoinspireyou.com, an everyday miracle. I am truly in awe of how God, through a series of circumstances, worked everything out, which led me to start writing weekly about God in the ordinary. God also used His ordinary circumstances to provide an editor via a simple comment on Facebook on a mutual friend's post.

It is refreshing to see God in the little details of life, performing His everyday miracles. Then our faith in Him will grow and grow, and, as our faith increases, we will learn to trust Him more. We might even see Him perform even greater miracles.

Keep your eyes and heart open to His everyday miracles.

REFLECTION:

What every day miracle have you recently experienced?
What bigger miracle have you seen God perform?

"Now a certain man was ill, Lazarus of Bethany, the village of Mary and her sister Martha. It was Mary who anointed the Lord with ointment and wiped his feet with her hair, whose brother Lazarus was ill. So the sisters sent to him, saying, 'Lord, he whom you love is ill.' But when Jesus heard it he said, 'This illness does not lead to death. It is for the glory of God, so that the Son of God may be glorified through it.'"
~ John 11:1-4 (ESV)

16

The Vast Ocean

When I was young, my family would vacation in North Wildwood, NJ, enjoying the beach and boardwalk. We always stayed in the same motel, The Flying Dutchman, usually with an ocean view room that was a short walk to the beach. Even as a child, I was sad when it was time to leave and return home. I wanted to stay there, where I could feel God's presence.

I have enjoyed sharing my love of the beach with my children through the years. It is still difficult when it is time to leave. I feel the glory and splendor of the Lord by the ocean. It is a wonder of His presence, where His awesome love and beauty flow forth.

The ocean is special to me because...

> I love to look out and see the miles and miles of vast ocean water, never seeing the beginning or the end of it.
> I marvel at the width and depth of the ocean's waters.
> it is amazing to think how the tides continually ebb and flow each day.
> I'm in awe of watching the waves, which are sometimes enormous and sometimes few and far between.
> I love to think about all the living creatures and things in the ocean waters, each having its own life pattern and serving God's purpose.
> of the beauty of the uncountable grains of sand in the ocean and on the beaches.

I am reminded of the Bible stories of Jesus and His disciples on the Sea of Galilee.

there is a peacefulness in listening as the waves soothe my soul.

"Who is like you, Lord God Almighty? You, Lord, are mighty, and your faithfulness surrounds you. You rule over the surging sea, when its waves mount up, you still them."
~ Psalm 89:8-9

One year, my family visited a place called Marco Island on the southwest coast of Florida. It was a beautiful place, and the water was calm with a blue-green hue. Being on the west coast provided stunning sunsets that glistened upon the ocean waters every night.

"The seas have lifted up, Lord, the seas have lifted up their voice; the seas have lifted up their pounding waves. Mightier than the thunder of the great waters, mightier than the breakers of the sea—the Lord on high is mighty."
~ Psalm 93:3-4

REFLECTION:

Where in nature do you feel closest to God's presence?
What is your favorite part about the vast ocean?

"How many are your works, O Lord! In wisdom you made them all; the earth is full of your creatures. There is the sea, vast and spacious, teeming with creatures beyond number—living things both large and small. May the glory of the Lord endure forever; may the Lord rejoice in his works—"
~ Psalm 104:24-25, 31

17

Everything Changes

"Everything changes…Nothing stays the same."

My mother frequently repeats this quote, yet I have wrestled with it, not wanting it to be true. Recently, as much as I dislike it, I have conceded that, indeed, it is the truth, and it is okay.

My disagreement comes from my way of thinking, which is, "Once a friend, why not always a friend?" After all, loyalty and faithfulness are good qualities, right? And like the saying, "If something isn't broken, why change it?"

Do you ever get into a routine with your daily activities and do the same thing at the same time every day or week? Routine sometimes brings comfort and peace. But *everything changes…nothing stays the same.*

Consider how the physical world God created was made to change:

> There are four seasons.
> The moon goes through changes daily.
> The sun rises and sets daily.
> The tides come and go throughout the day.
> Sometimes the clouds bring rain to water the earth.
> Animals are born and die.
> There are seasons of planting and harvesting crops.

Christine M. Fisher

Consider how the people God created change:

Our physical bodies are constantly changing—we start out as babies, and we change as we grow into toddlers, teenagers, young adults, middle age, and old age.

Our brains are continually learning and evolving, starting out with little knowledge but learning more and more as we mature.

There are different seasons where we may have to embrace change.

A season...

to be a child, learning from our parents.
to be a young adult where we learn more and figure out our purpose in this world.
to raise a family while helping our children find their way.
of letting our children go to explore their own lives.
of empty nest-ness.
of retirement.

Each of these seasons may bring different people into our lives. Sometimes people may stick throughout all seasons, but it is more likely that people are part of our lives for a particular season. Each of these seasons bring different events, and the events do change—they come and go in our lives.

As I was reflecting on the seasons and changes, it occurred to me that maybe God allows **all** these changes to show us the beauty that takes place.

Think about a caterpillar—it even goes through changes during its life cycle. What do those changes provide?

Growth

And what does that growth produce in the caterpillar?

A beautiful butterfly!

A butterfly that is ready to use its wings to soar through this beautiful world that God created.

Isn't that a great parallel in our lives? We start out as babies, dependent on our parents for everything. But each day brings change in us, both physically and in character, causing us to grow. Each different season of our lives contributes to new growth in us and changes us. It changes us so that we grow into the beautiful creation God has purposed for us. We become like the butterfly and get to use our wings to soar through this amazing world God created.

I do believe, though, that there is one flaw with the statement, *"Everything changes…Nothing stays the same."*

A more accurate statement of truth would be: *"Everything changes; nothing stays the same except for God, our Creator."*

Isn't it amazing to consider that God, His love, and His faithfulness never change; they are always constant?

Consider these verses:

> *"For I the Lord do not change; therefore you, O*
> *children of Jacob, are not consumed."*
> ~ Malachi 3:6 (ESV)

"Every good gift and every perfect gift is from above, coming down from the Father of lights, with whom there is no variation or shadow due to change."
~ James 1:17 (ESV)

Christine M. Fisher

"The steadfast love of the Lord never ceases;
his mercies never come to an end."
~ Lamentations 3:22 (ESV)

"God is not man, that he should lie, or a son of man, that
he should change his mind. Has he said, and will he not
do it? Or has he spoken, and will he not fulfill it?"
~ Numbers 23:19 (ESV)

REFLECTION:

What has produced the greatest growth in your faith journey?
How are you growing in the current season you are experiencing?

"So we do not lose heart. Though our outer self is wasting away, our inner
self is being renewed day by day. For this light momentary affliction is
preparing for us an eternal weight of glory beyond all comparison..."
~ 2 Corinthians 4:16-17 (ESV)

18

Beautiful Blessing

Recently, my mailbox contained an unexpected gift from a woman in Tennessee. The note explained she was doing art therapy and she added, "When I finished painting this rock, I noticed it was in the shape of a heart and thought of you, and God whispered, 'That's who I wanted you to paint it for.' Isn't He so good?"

A beautiful blessing ~ a heart rock

She knows how God sends me hearts to remind me of His great love and to share that love with others. I was not familiar with the verse written on the back,

"The man of God came up and told the king of Israel, 'This is what the Lord says: "Because the Arameans think the Lord is a god of

Christine M. Fisher

the hills and not a god of the valleys, I will deliver this vast army
into your hands, and you will know that I am the Lord"""
~ 1 Kings 20:28

In this scripture, the Israelites were in a battle with the Arameans who thought Israel's God would only be victorious if the battle took place in the hills. They soon found out the error in their thinking, as the man of God shared the Lord's message. This verse reminds me how sovereign God truly is. He is the Lord of everything in nature and on earth. Everything is under His dominion.

Gazing at the beauty of this masterpiece, I could not help but marvel at the colors on this rock. The mountain range in the background reminded me of the Judean Desert I experienced in the Holy Land. I emailed her to tell her that pink and purple happen to be my favorite colors, which she did not know. I ended the email with "I can't stop smiling."

I will share excerpts from her return email that confirm the Scripture about the sovereignty of God:

"And He just keeps on. Now **I** can't quit smiling. I just had a really good laugh with God that totally warmed my heart. I could just feel Him hugging me. Anyway, after I finished it, I wanted to seal it for protection so the colors wouldn't fade or get chipped away. So, I decided to put a coat of polyurethane on it. As I was painting it on, I started noticing that it was mixing with my colors, even though they were dry. I went into a panic! I got so upset with myself and thought I had messed it up completely. I grabbed my other brush and started trying to remove as much of the poly as I could. After it dried, I thought, 'Well, it doesn't look as bad as I thought it would. I guess it will be okay.' Yes, God is so good. He knew exactly what He was doing, from start to finish, on something as simple as a rock. I feel so humbled. I can't quit smiling either."

Heart rock before polyurethane

"And we know that God causes everything to work together for the good of those who love God and are called according to his purpose for them."
~ Romans 8:28 (NLT)

I thought of my favorite Bible verse (Romans 8:28) in relation to the story my friend shared. She thought adding the polyurethane ruined the colors she had envisioned for the rock. Little did she know that God was using it to be the perfect color and look for me. God even uses rocks to show His sovereignty reigns as His perfect orchestrations light our path when we continue to love and serve Him.

Seeing the before and after pictures of this masterpiece made me reflect on how we become beautiful masterpieces when we allow God to control the paintbrush in our lives. God produces the sparkle—the shine that makes us radiant with His presence and joy.

Christine M. Fisher

May you be reminded of…

>God's sovereignty in your life.
>the importance of loving God with all your heart.
>how God works out all life's circumstances for your good.
>letting God control the paintbrush in your life.
>shining the radiance of God's presence and joy.

REFLECTION:

What was a meaningful blessing you received from someone?
What special orchestration did God provide in your life?

>*"And the Lord said, 'Behold, there is a place by me where you shall stand on the rock, and while my glory passes by I will put you in a cleft of the rock, and I will cover you with my hand until I have passed by.'"*
>*- Exodus 33:21-22 (ESV)*

19

Butterflies

While at Lake Ontario, writing and communing with the Lord and His creation, there were two monarch butterflies flying around, keeping me company.

I reflected on what happens when a butterfly emerges. Once a butterfly egg hatches, it becomes a caterpillar, a creature that can only creep and crawl along. After lots of food and two to four weeks as a caterpillar, it turns into a chrysalis, or pupa. The caterpillar undergoes great transformation here, which turns the caterpillar into a butterfly. Butterflies reflect their beauty as they fly all over God's creation.

Aren't there parallels between butterflies and our lives in Christ? Don't our lives go through transformation that leads us to Christ? We become new creations in Christ.

> *"Therefore, if anyone is in Christ, he is a new creation. The old has passed away; behold, the new has come."*
> ~ 2 Corinthians 5:17 (ESV)

Once we come to Christ, there is ongoing growth and transformation that continues throughout our lives.

> *"Do not conform to the pattern of this world but be transformed by the renewing of your mind. Then you will be able to test and approve what God's will is—his good, pleasing and perfect will."*
> ~ Romans 12:2

Christine M. Fisher

At first, we crawl around trying to find our way, but we end up soaring with the Lord.

> *"But those who hope in the Lord will renew their strength.*
> *They will soar on wings like eagles; they will run and not*
> *grow weary, they will walk and not be faint."*
> ~ Isaiah 40:31

After working from home for two years, I felt like a butterfly when I had to return to the workplace. It seemed the time at home was a time of personal growth in Scripture and prayer, providing me with more alone time with the Lord. Having the opportunity to work from home, unable to do my usual ministries because of the pandemic, I was inspired to publish two books. During that two year period, I was being transformed from the inside out. I have emerged, ready to spread my wings and fly to whatever God has in store.

Wasn't Jesus' life like a caterpillar that turned into a butterfly for you and me? Just as a caterpillar makes a cocoon and seems to be dead, so Jesus died on the cross for you and me. His lifeless body was taken down from the cross and placed in a tomb. Three days later, He rose from the dead.

> *"I passed on to you what was most important and what had*
> *also been passed on to me. Christ died for our sins, just as*
> *the Scriptures said. He was buried, and he was raised from*
> *the dead on the third day, just as the Scriptures said."*
> ~ 1 Corinthians 15:3-4 (NLT)

As I was sitting with the lake in front of me, I watched a butterfly on the water's edge. He was perched on the dry part of a rock, basking in the sunshine, not fazed by the waves of the lake. When he moved, he landed on the next rock with his wings slightly open and then displayed the beauty of his wingspan before eventually flying around in freedom.

Shouldn't we be more like that butterfly...

NOT FAZED BY THE STORMS IN LIFE?

"Whoever dwells in the shelter of the Most High will rest in the shadow of the Almighty. I will say of the Lord, 'He is my refuge and my fortress, my God, in whom I trust.'"
~ Psalm 91:1-2

READY TO MOVE ON TO THE NEXT PLACE WHEN IT'S TIME?

"I will instruct you and teach you in the way you should go; I will counsel you with my loving eye on you."
~ Psalm 32:8

DISPLAYING THE BEAUTY OF OUR LIVES THAT GOD HAS MADE?

"Thank you for making me so wonderfully complex! Your workmanship is marvelous—how well I know it."
~ Psalm 139:14 (NLT)

Be encouraged to be like a beautiful butterfly by...

letting God transform you with beauty and grace.
continually growing in the Lord.
soaring with the Lord.

being at peace.
knowing God is leading you.
embracing the uniqueness of how God made you.

Enjoy the freedom of spreading your wings and sharing the beauty of your life with everyone, giving glory to God.

Christine M. Fisher

A few fun butterfly facts:

Caterpillars have eight pairs of legs. The first three pairs, the thoracic legs, are jointed with hooks and will become the butterfly's legs.

Butterflies use their feet to taste.

Butterflies actually have four wings, not two.

The average lifespan of an adult butterfly is roughly three to four weeks. At least one species of butterfly lives for approximately twenty-four hours, while some migratory butterflies can survive for nearly eight months.

REFLECTION:

What transformation in growth have you recently experienced?
What characteristic of a butterfly do you need to be more like?

"Shout joyful praises to God, all the earth! Sing about the glory of his name! Tell the world how glorious he is."
~ Psalm 66:1-2 (NLT)

20

Resilient

As I sat in solitude with the lake before me, it was mesmerizing watching some geese bob up and down, led by the buoyancy of the water. These same geese, a few minutes later, came to the shore and waddled onto the dry ground, looking for something to feast on. After getting their fill, they took to the air, flying in different formations high in the sky and talking with each other.

While watching the geese, I thought about how God made them resilient so they could adapt easily to different environments. For me, resilient means being flexible, adapting to different situations and hardships in our lives. When we are resilient, we are also open to continual change. I believe God was showing me how good it is to be resilient, just as the geese are.

How important it is to adapt to whatever life hands us, to rebound, and to make the most of everything.

Paul, formerly known as Saul (Acts 9), is a great example from the Bible of someone resilient. He went from being one of the worst persecutors of Christians to being the chief preacher to the Gentiles, allowing salvation for **all** people. In his travels, Paul was often beaten and suffered persecution for preaching the good news. His resiliency caused him to carry on despite the hardships. (Read the Acts of the Apostles, and you will find many stories from Paul's life where he was resilient.)

"But Jews came from Antioch and Iconium, and having persuaded the crowds, they stoned Paul and dragged him out of the city, supposing that he was dead. But when the disciples gathered about him, he rose up and entered the city, and on the next day he went on with Barnabas to Derbe."
~ Acts 14:19-20 (ESV)

Paul continuously preached from town to town as he shared the gospel. He first shared with the Jewish people, but when he ran into opposition, he started sharing the good news with the Gentiles. He was resilient enough to keep sharing with those who would listen and come to know Christ.

"When Silas and Timothy came from Macedonia, Paul devoted himself exclusively to preaching, testifying to the Jews that Jesus was the Messiah. But when they opposed Paul and became abusive, he shook out his clothes in protest and said to them, 'Your blood be on your own heads! I am innocent of it. From now on I will go to the Gentiles.'"
~ Acts 18:5-6

Paul continuously followed God's will and was willing to sacrifice his life for the cause of spreading the gospel. He was resilient enough to do whatever it took to follow God.

"When we heard this, we and the people there urged him not to go up to Jerusalem. Then Paul answered, 'What are you doing, weeping and breaking my heart? For I am ready not only to be imprisoned but even to die in Jerusalem for the name of the Lord Jesus.' And since he would not be persuaded, we ceased and said, 'Let the will of the Lord be done.'"
~ Acts 21:12-14 (ESV)

Why was Paul able to be so resilient?

Paul came to know that God is sovereign.

Paul knew he was safe in God's hands, who works everything out for our good.

Paul knew that God provided all he needed, even with the many hardships he endured.

Paul knew he could trust God completely.

As we walk this earth, can we, too, strive to follow Paul's example of being resilient?

No matter what happens, can we be resilient, knowing God is sovereign?

Applying these same principles Paul applied to his life will help us be resilient. Be encouraged to trust God with everything that happens in your life.

REFLECTION:

In what area do you need to grow in resilience?

Do you need to trust God more?

> *"The Lord will rescue me from every evil attack and*
> *will bring me safely to his heavenly kingdom.*
> *To him be glory for ever and ever. Amen."*
> ~ 2 Timothy 4:18

21

Always With You

One of my holy places is a retreat house that overlooks a beautiful lake. It is a two hour drive each way, and sometimes I experience the sunrise on my drive to the retreat house, through my rearview mirror, and the sunset on my drive back home, through the rearview mirror.

With the beauty of the sunrise and sunset at my back, it seemed God's presence was following me, leading me from behind. His illuminating light was guiding my path throughout the day. It was a beautiful visual of a great truth, reminding me of the Lord's presence experienced by the Israelites.

> *"They marched for three days after leaving the mountain of the Lord, with the Ark of the Lord's Covenant moving ahead of them to show them where to stop and rest. As they moved on each day, the cloud of the Lord hovered over them."*
> ~ Numbers 10:33-34 (NLT)

The Israelites were traveling from Sinai to the land of Canaan, which was the Promised Land. The Lord's presence was in the cloud and determined when the Israelites would set out and stop traveling for the day. God's presence was guiding them and was always with them.

> *"You go before me and follow me. You place your hand of blessing on my head. Such knowledge is too wonderful for me, too great for me to understand! I can never escape from your Spirit! I can never get away from your presence!"*
> ~ Psalm 139:5-7 (NLT)

Because of God's great love for us, He goes before us and even follows us. Everywhere we go, God is there. God is omnipresent, meaning He is present everywhere, all the time. Our minds find this hard to comprehend. Jesus sent us the Holy Spirit after He ascended to God. Not only is God with us, but God lives in us.

Be reminded, no matter what you face...

God is present with and in you.
God is before you and following you.
God is leading and guiding you.
God is omnipresent, so you can never escape Him.

REFLECTION:

When did you experience God truly guiding you?
How do you see God's presence shining through you?

"But the whole community began to talk about stoning Joshua and Caleb. Then the glorious presence of the Lord appeared to all the Israelites at the Tabernacle."
~ Numbers 14:10 (NLT)

22

GPS Saga

I have a love-hate relationship with the GPS. My youngest son and I had a harrowing experience when we trusted our GPS rather than Google Maps.

We were headed to a house about a half hour away. According to the GPS, we were going to arrive five minutes ahead of the scheduled meeting time. It was evening, so it was dark out, and the last four miles of our journey were on unfamiliar roads. We trusted the directions given by the GPS, thinking it knew the fastest and best route to take. The GPS said we were 1.7 miles from our destination, so following the instructions, we turned on a curvy, dirt road where there were no streetlights. Before long, the road seemed to narrow, became hilly, and was covered in snow and ice. With snow tires on the car, we managed pretty well, but with one mile left, my son suggested that we turn around and find the road we had seen on Google Maps earlier in the day.

Once confronted with the snowy road, a sense of fear enveloped us for a few minutes, but we tried to set that aside so we could figure out how to get back to civilization. Our only option was to try to back down until we could find a spot to turn around. We slowly backed down, trying to steer the car carefully and not go off the road. A lifesaver was my van's backup camera. I do not know how we would have managed without it, especially with the curves of the road in the pitch dark. We did eventually find a spot to turn around, and we were able to go the Google Maps way, arriving thirty-five minutes later than expected.

This experience made me think about our life journey on earth.

A reminder that…

> we need to put our trust only in God and His Word; our faith is in Him alone.
> sometimes we need to backtrack if we start going the wrong way.
> slow and steady is the way.
> we may plan our journey, but ultimately, the Lord is in control.
> God is greater than our fear; faith over fear.
> we find shelter on the solid ground of Jesus, our rock.

REFLECTION:

In what situation did you trust the Lord to get you through?
How did you see God control an event in your life?

> *"How amazing are the deeds of the Lord! All who delight*
> *in him should ponder them. Everything he does reveals his*
> *glory and majesty. His righteousness never fails."*
> ~ Psalm 111:2-3 (NLT)

Christine M. Fisher

23

Calm Waters

As I was observing Lake Ontario's calm water, I began to think about the parallels between the water, waves, wind, and God in our lives.

No matter if our lives are stormy, tumultuous, or calm,
no matter what way the wind is blowing,
the one constant is God,
the anchor to keep us grounded.

What can we learn from Bible verses referencing calm waters?

> *"You faithfully answer our prayers with awesome deeds, O God our savior. You are the hope of everyone on earth, even those who sail on distant seas. You formed the mountains by your power and armed yourself with mighty strength. You quieted the raging oceans with their pounding waves and silenced the shouting of the nations. Those who live at the ends of the earth stand in awe of your wonders. From where the sun rises to where it sets, you inspire shouts of joy."*
> ~ Psalm 65:5-8 (NLT)

What a beautiful psalm of praise to God. The psalmist shares how God is the One who silences the raging waters, both literally and figuratively, in our lives. He calms the waters. How important it is to continually praise the Lord, be in awe of His wonders, and declare His lordship with shouts of joy.

> *"'Lord, help!' they cried in their trouble, and he saved them from their distress. He calmed the storm to a whisper and stilled the*

waves. What a blessing was that stillness as he brought them safely into harbor! Let them praise the Lord for his great love and for the wonderful things he has done for them. Let them exalt him publicly before the congregation and before the leaders of the nation."
~ Psalm 107:28-32 (NLT)

How do we get calm waters in our lives? We can cry out to the Lord in times of trouble. He can turn the storm into a whisper and calm the waves. We can trust Him to bring us to a place of safety as He guides our footsteps, always with us. The psalmist reminds us to see God's great love and to exalt Him in all things, even if the storm isn't calmed the way we think it should be.

"The Lord is my shepherd; I shall not want. He makes me lie down in green pastures. He leads me beside still waters. He restores my soul. He leads me in paths of righteousness for his name's sake."
~ Psalm 23:1-3 (ESV)

Where does the Lord lead us? The Lord, being our Good Shepherd, leads us to the calm, still waters of our lives. Even in the raging storms, He is the One who supplies moments of refreshment, peace, and even joy, as we know He provides what we need.

Even in calm waters, boats still need anchors to provide stability to steady the boat and stop it from drifting. It is the same in the calm waters of our lives. We still need our anchor, Jesus, and the hope He provides.

"We put our hope in the Lord. He is our help and our shield. In him our hearts rejoice, for we trust in his holy name. Let your unfailing love surround us, Lord, for our hope is in you alone. I will praise the Lord at all times. I will constantly speak his praises."
~ Psalm 33:20-22, 34:1 (NLT)

Christine M. Fisher

Our hope, Jesus, is our help and shield. He is the One who calms the waters of our lives. When we embrace His unfailing love that is always with us, we are able to trust Him more and praise Him at all times. What a mighty Lord and Savior we have.

In the calm waters of life, be encouraged to...

> be in awe of God.
> remember that God helps you in your distress.
> experience Him restoring your soul.
> remain attached to the anchor of your soul, Jesus, in the calm waters.

No matter if our lives are stormy, tumultuous, or calm,
> no matter what way the wind is blowing,
>> the one constant is God,
>>> the anchor to keep us grounded.

REFLECTION:

When did Jesus calm the waters in your life?
How does your faith serve as your anchor?

"In his kindness God called you to share in his eternal glory by means of Christ Jesus. So after you have suffered a little while, he will restore, support, and strengthen you, and he will place you on a firm foundation."
~ 1 Peter 5:10 (NLT)

24

The Pearl

THE WORLD WAS MY OYSTER
BUT WHERE WAS THE PEARL?

Hearing these words from the musical *Annie* inspired me to share them. At the end of the production, there was a short talk about Jesus that connected it more with our Christian faith. You might know the story of little orphan Annie, who was left at an orphanage in NYC when she was young and eventually adopted by a billionaire, Mr. Warbucks.

THE WORLD WAS MY OYSTER
BUT WHERE WAS THE PEARL?[1]

are words from *Something Was Missing* sung by Mr. Warbucks.

Though we know that Mr. Warbucks was referring to Annie as the pearl, I believe this song is a very fitting parallel in our lives in regard to our relationship with…

Jesus being the pearl in our lives.

Even with all the money in the world…

Even with being the most famous and sought-after person in this world…

At first, we don't even know, but after while we realize…
SOMETHING WAS MISSING. SOMEONE WAS MISSING.

Even if we give the most eloquent speeches…

    Even if we have universities named after us…

        SOMETHING WAS MISSING. SOMEONE WAS MISSING.

There is someone who wants us…

    There is someone who needs us to live for Him…

        There is someone who needs us just as we are…

            There is someone who loves imperfect us…

      THE WORLD WAS MY OYSTER
      BUT WHERE WAS THE PEARL?

Who dreamed we could be free…

    And find something that was missing…

        Yes, there is nothing like you…

            SOMETHING WAS MISSING. SOMEONE WAS MISSING.

      THE WORLD WAS MY OYSTER
      BUT WHERE WAS THE PEARL?

This world we live in can symbolize our **oyster.**

    But have you found the **pearl**…

        the pearl that is **Jesus**?

Isn't it amazing to think about a natural pearl that one finds? Aren't they one of the purest, most beautiful gems formed by God's handiwork?

A pearl is perfect just as it is. Human hands don't have to do anything to make it better in appearance or more radiant. That's what makes the pearl so valuable and precious, just as it is.

Is Jesus all of that in your life?

  Your pearl, Jesus, is the most valuable gemstone in your life.

   This treasure is far beyond any other in this world; nothing compares.

    Let Him radiate through you.

REFLECTION:

Who or what is the true pearl in your life?
How do you share Jesus with others?

*"And the king answered and said, 'Is not this great
Babylon, which I have built by my mighty power as a
royal residence and for the glory of my majesty?'"*
~ Daniel 4:30 (ESV)

25

In Awe

"Who is like You among the gods, O Lord? Who is like You,
majestic in holiness, awesome in praises, working wonders?"
~ Exodus 15:11 (NASB)

I am in awe of the Lord and His amazing creation. One does not have to look far to see Him at work creating such a wonderful world, which surrounds us as well as all the inhabitants. All of nature is awe-inspiring. It was one of the first places I connected with God in a powerful way.

I saw a video of a plant that made me stop and think—what an awesome God we have who could form such amazing creations. My brother-in-law was visiting Thailand, when he saw a mimosa pudica plant growing in a garden.

Encyclopedia Britannica says: "The mimosa pudica plant, also nicknamed the humble plant, responds to touch and other stimulation by rapidly closing its leaves and drooping. The plant's unusually quick response to touch is due to rapid water release from specialized cells located at the bases of leaflet and leaf stalks. The leaves reopen in several minutes, and it is thought that this adaptation is a defense against browsing herbivores who may be startled by the movement. In addition to its response to physical stimuli, the leaves also droop in response to darkness and reopen with daylight, a phenomenon known as nyctinastic movement."

It is awe-inspiring to learn about the special attributes of the mimosa pudica plant, created by God.

*"Let the heavens rejoice, let the earth be glad; let the sea resound,
and all that is in it. Let the fields be jubilant, and everything
in them; let all the trees of the forest sing for joy."*
~ Psalm 96:11-12

One of the most fascinating birds in Tanzania is the gorgeous, bright yellow vitelline masked weaver. True, hard-working artisans, the males are responsible for building the nests, sometimes up to twenty-five each season, which takes about nine to fourteen hours each to complete. Once completed, they will display it to the females, hoping to attract one to their humble abode. If a picky female approves, she will line the interior with soft grass and feathers and lay two to five eggs, which only she incubates. My friend watched a male building a nest and was amazed how he used his beak and feet to weave the grasses together. A skilled nest builder, he worked tirelessly to build the perfect love nest.

It is awe-inspiring to learn how this bird painstakingly takes so much time to build such a beautiful nest.

*"But ask the animals, and they will teach you, or the birds in the
sky, and they will tell you; or speak to the earth, and it will teach
you, or let the fish in the sea inform you. Which of all these does
not know that the hand of the Lord has done this? In his hand
is the life of every creature and the breath of all mankind."*
~ Job 12:7-10

Being fascinated with the look of the pelican eel, further research yielded that its mouth is much bigger than its actual body, yet it has tiny teeth. The pelican eel can swallow a fish much bigger than the eel itself due to its loosely hinged mouth. Another unique attribute of the pelican eel is that it does not have pelvic fins, swim bladders, or scales. Movement is provided via the whip-like tail, where numerous tentacles can be found at the base of the tail. These tentacles glow pink and give off occasional bright red flashes.

Learning about the unique features of the pelican eel makes me in awe of God, the Creator of all things.

> *"In his hand are the depths of the earth, and the mountain peaks belong to him. The sea is his, for he made it, and his hands formed the dry land."*
> ~ Psalm 95:4-5

REFLECTION:

What creature amazes you?
Have you reflected on the fact that you are one of God's finest creations?

> *"He is your glory and he is your God, who has done these great and awesome things for you which your eyes have seen."*
> ~ Deuteronomy 10:21 (NASB)

26

Come Away With Me

"Then, because so many people were coming and going that
they did not even have a chance to eat, he said to them, 'Come
with me by yourselves to a quiet place and get some rest.'"
~ Mark 6:31

Have you had the benefit of getting away from the busyness of life to spend time being with the Lord and enjoying the blessings all around?

Maybe...

> it was on your vacation where you experienced God's presence in the beauty of the environment that surrounded you.
> you had the privilege of attending a retreat where you had a close encounter with God.
> you took time to experience Him in peace and solitude.

One summer, I attended a three-day retreat where I could commune with the Lord in a reflective way. Spending time with like-minded people is always inspiring, as we share our faith with others. It provides opportunities for making new friends in the Lord and learning from others' stories.

"Be still and know I am God..."
~ Psalm 46:10 (ESV)

It is enlightening to read the many Scripture passages that show how many times Jesus took time to be alone with God, His Father, getting away from everyone.

*"One of those days Jesus went out to a mountainside
to pray and spent the night praying to God."*
~ Luke 6:12

"But Jesus often withdrew to lonely places and prayed."
~ Luke 5:16

*"Very early in the morning, while it was still dark, Jesus got up, left
the house and went off to a solitary place, where he prayed."*
~ Mark 1:35

*"After he had dismissed them, he went up on a
mountainside by himself to pray..."*
~ Matthew 14:23

I encourage you to take advantage of opportunities to attend a retreat or gathering that will strengthen your faith. It will help you refocus and concentrate on the important things in life. Even taking time daily to go to your quiet prayer corner and commune with the Lord will enrich your spirit and get you in tune with the Creator.

A powerful story of Jesus taking time to pray was right before He was arrested. Jesus knew the most important thing He could do was pray to His Father.

*"Then Jesus went with his disciples to a place called Gethsemane, and he
said to them, 'Sit here while I go over there and pray.' He took Peter and
the two sons of Zebedee along with him, and he began to be sorrowful and
troubled. Then he said to them, 'My soul is overwhelmed with sorrow to the
point of death. Stay here and keep watch with me.' Going a little farther,
he fell with his face to the ground and prayed, 'My Father, if it is possible,
may this cup be taken from me. Yet not as I will, but as you will.' Then he
returned to his disciples and found them sleeping. 'Couldn't you men keep*

watch with me for one hour?' he asked Peter. 'Watch and pray so that you will not fall into temptation. The spirit is willing, but the flesh is weak.' He went away a second time and prayed, 'My Father, if it is not possible for this cup to be taken away unless I drink it, may your will be done.' When he came back, he again found them sleeping, because their eyes were heavy. So he left them and went away once more and prayed the third time, saying the same thing. Then he returned to the disciples and said to them, 'Are you still sleeping and resting? Look, the hour has come, and the Son of Man is delivered into the hands of sinners. Rise! Let us go! Here comes my betrayer!'"
~ Matthew 26:36-46

Father, may we grow daily to be like your Son, Jesus, taking time to pray and become one with you. Amen.

REFLECTION:

Where do you go to be still with the Lord?
Is it time for you to step out in faith to attend a retreat?

"When the priests withdrew from the Holy Place, the cloud filled the temple of the Lord. And the priests could not perform their service because of the cloud, for the glory of the Lord filled his temple."
~ 1 Kings 8:10-11

Christine M. Fisher

27

Uncharted Waters

Have you ever been fearful of a new beginning in your life?
Has fear stopped you from taking a new step in life?

Maybe it was related to something God was calling you to do, but you weren't sure how.

Maybe it was not knowing what to expect that was difficult.

Maybe you were too scared to take that leap of faith because you didn't know what you would find.

When I was traveling solo on a four hour drive, thoughts of being stuck in a traffic delay made me think about uncharted waters in our lives. The prior day, I observed what seemed like miles of traffic backed up on the opposite side of the road due to construction. I mentioned the traffic I had seen to a friend, who, in turn, suggested I consider an alternate route home, which I did.

Off I went into uncharted waters, a route I had never taken before. Much to my surprise, it was a beautiful, peaceful drive through some country roads. I had no idea where it was taking me, especially when it appeared I only had forty minutes left on the trip and should have already been back on the highway. Rather than panicking, I continued listening and singing with my Christian music and trusting the GPS.

I started to think about the uncharted waters I was experiencing and how they apply to different events in our lives…

I kept moving forward, following the GPS directions.
It was an opportunity to trust I was doing the right thing.
I got to see a different view of the area that I hadn't seen before.
It really was okay to take a new path.
I knew the important thing was getting to the destination.
A new adventure can be exciting.

The uncharted waters trip seemed like it would never end. When at last it was time to get back on the highway, there was a closed road sign **before** the ramp I needed to take. The only option was to get on the highway that took me in the opposite direction from home, whose ramp was before the closed road. There was really nothing I could do except go with the flow of the traffic. My adventure brought me encouragement to remember that uncharted waters are really okay; I hope it provides the same for you. What do we really have to fear with the Lord at our side?

REFLECTION:

What uncharted waters have you recently experienced?
What did you learn from the uncharted waters?

"For the Lord God is our sun and our shield. He gives us grace and glory. The Lord will withhold no good thing from those who do what is right."
~ Psalm 84:11 (NLT)

Christine M. Fisher

28

Fall Time Beauty

We can experience God's presence in many different ways. When I stop to consider that God made this world and everything in it, I am in awe. It seems natural, then, that we can experience His presence in everything. Can you think of times when you personally encountered God while reading Scripture, in nature, in the people you meet, and in times of worship and prayer?

One fall day, as I sat in my chair on a sandy beach, ironically at a place called Promised Land State Park in Greentown, PA, I was immersed in the beauty of creation that surrounded me. In the Old Testament, the Promised Land was for the Israelites, the land of Canaan, which represented for them a land flowing with milk and honey.

> *"The Lord said, 'I have indeed seen the misery of my people* [the Israelites] *in Egypt. I have heard them crying out because of their slave drivers, and I am concerned about their suffering. So I have come down to rescue them from the hand of the Egyptians and to bring them up out of that land into a good and spacious land, a land flowing with milk and honey—the home of the Canaanites, Hittites, Amorites, Perizzites, Hivites and Jebusites.'"*
> ~ Exodus 3:7-8

In God's boundless compassion, He saw the oppression His chosen people, the Israelites, were experiencing at the hands of the Egyptians. He led them to Canaan, the Promised Land, which symbolized a land flowing with milk and honey. The Promised Land was a good and spacious place where they could live in freedom. The milk and honey symbolized goodness, wealth, agricultural richness, and happiness.

While I was at the park, I felt I had also found the land flowing with milk and honey. The many trees surrounding the lake were vibrant with color. There were beautiful shades of orange, red, and yellow that took my breath away. The sky was pure blue with no clouds. I smiled to see the water looking like it was dancing with the sunlight reflecting on it, making it sparkle.

As I was alternating between sitting and standing, I looked toward my left foot to see a perfectly shaped heart stone in the sand. I laughed at God's reminder of His great love for me and His desire for me to love others with the same love.

> *"God showed how much he loved us by sending his one and only Son into the world so that we might have eternal life through him. This is real love—not that we loved God, but that he loved us and sent his Son as a sacrifice to take away our sins. Dear friends, since God loved us that much, we surely ought to love each other."*
> ~ 1 John 4:9-11 (NLT)

God's love is so great for each one of us that He sent Jesus to earth to die for our sins, granting eternal life to all who believe in Jesus. We need to share that same unconditional love with all we meet.

What was most interesting about this heart is that when I took the stone out of the sand, it was not heart shaped. A friend with whom I shared the pictures said, "This rock needed the sand to look like a heart. It is just like us. We need Jesus to help us see how, at times, we have hidden our hearts below all the other stuff in our lives."

Christine M. Fisher

"Once a religious leader asked Jesus this question: 'Good Teacher, what should I do to inherit eternal life?' 'Why do you call me good?' Jesus asked him. 'Only God is truly good. But to answer your question, you know the commandments: "You must not commit adultery. You must not murder. You must not steal. You must not testify falsely. Honor your father and mother."' The man replied, 'I've obeyed all these commandments since I was young.' When Jesus heard his answer, he said, 'There is still one thing you haven't done. Sell all your possessions and give the money to the poor, and you will have treasure in heaven. Then come, follow me.' But when the man heard this he became very sad, for he was very rich."
~ Luke 18:18-23 (NLT)

This religious leader's heart was hidden beneath the things of this world that often get in our way. He had kept the commandments, but the one thing he had not been able to do was follow Jesus with his whole heart. His heart was focused on the material treasure, which he was not willing to part with. Jesus called this leader to follow Him and put Him first in his life. It appears he was not willing to do that.

Be encouraged to…

> see the Promised Land flowing with milk and honey that God provides in your life.
> be aware of the ways God is reminding you of His great love.
> be aware of the ways God is calling you to love others with His love.
> see how Jesus is calling you to draw your heart closer to Him above all the other things in your life.

REFLECTION:

Where have you experienced God's presence recently?
How can you follow Jesus more deeply with your whole heart?

"Glory in his holy name; let the hearts of those who seek the Lord rejoice."
~ 1 Chronicles 16:10

29

Advice From a Tree

Isn't it incredible to reflect on the fact that God has made everything and orchestrated the working together of it all? God is truly so amazing. Isn't it also inspiring to see how, as human beings, we can learn lessons from everything God created, including both nature and people?

What wonderful advice the trees teach us about our relationship with God and others.

STAND TALL AND PROUD.

> *"Only let your manner of life be worthy of the gospel of Christ,*
> *so that whether I come and see you or am absent, I may hear*
> *of you that you are standing firm in one spirit, with one*
> *mind striving side by side for the faith of the gospel."*
> ~ Philippians 1:27 (ESV)

We can stand tall and proud like the mighty trees when we daily live out the gospel of Jesus Christ. The gospel is sharing the good news of Jesus, who came to earth, died, was resurrected, ascended to heaven, and is now seated next to God. It is Jesus who, when we put our faith in Him, sets us free from our sins because of His victory over the cross. We have the privilege of walking with other disciples on our journey to spend eternity in heaven and to help us stand firm in our faith.

What is one thing you do that helps you stand firm in your faith?

GO OUT ON A LIMB.

"Jesus entered Jericho and was passing through. A man was there by the name of Zacchaeus; he was a chief tax collector and was wealthy. He wanted to see who Jesus was, but because he was short he could not see over the crowd. So he ran ahead and climbed a sycamore-fig tree to see him, since Jesus was coming that way. When Jesus reached the spot, he looked up and said to him, 'Zacchaeus, come down immediately. I must stay at your house today.' So he came down at once and welcomed him gladly All the people saw this and began to mutter, 'He has gone to be the guest of a sinner.' But Zacchaeus stood up and said to the Lord, 'Look, Lord! Here and now I give half of my possessions to the poor, and if I have cheated anybody out of anything, I will pay back four times the amount.' Jesus said to him, 'Today salvation has come to this house, because this man, too, is a son of Abraham. For the Son of Man came to seek and to save the lost.'"
~ Luke 19:1-10

Zacchaeus was an important tax collector who made people pay more than their fair share of taxes. Despite his sin, he became a role model for us. He was short in stature and heard about Jesus coming to town. Zacchaeus physically went out on a limb to get a glimpse of Jesus. His encounter with Jesus changed the trajectory of his life as he repented of his wrongdoing and repaid people.

How do you go out on a limb for Jesus?

REMEMBER YOUR ROOTS.

"And now, just as you accepted Christ Jesus as your Lord, you must continue to follow him. Let your roots grow down into him, and let your lives be built on him. Then your faith will grow strong in the truth you were taught, and you will overflow with thankfulness."
~ Colossians 2:6-7 (NLT)

Christine M. Fisher

Once we accept Jesus as our personal Lord and Savior, we need to continue following Him faithfully each day. When we do this, the roots of our faith will become stronger as we grow in trust and gratitude and walk hand-in-hand with Him. We should never forget the root of our faith, which is Jesus.

Are your roots deep in the ground, or do you need to make some changes to be grounded more in Jesus?

DRINK PLENTY OF WATER.

"On the last day of the feast, the great day, Jesus stood up and cried out, 'If anyone thirsts, let him come to me and drink. Whoever believes in me, as the Scripture has said, "Out of his heart will flow rivers of living water."'"
~ John 7:37-38 (ESV)

For trees to grow big and strong, they need water to sustain them as well as sunshine to help them grow. Jesus is our living water that brings joy and peace to our spirits. He is the only thing that can satisfy our hunger and thirst. As we are filled with living water, it begins to flow from our hearts into the lives of others.

How deep is the living water in your heart?

BE CONTENT WITH YOUR NATURAL BEAUTY.

"Let your true beauty come from your inner personality, not a focus on the external. For lasting beauty comes from a gentle and peaceful spirit, which is precious in God's sight and is much more important than the outward adornment of elaborate hair, jewelry, and fine clothes."
~ 1 Peter 3:3-4 (TPT)

Isn't it amazing to see trees that have different colored leaves? Think about the trees that grow on the hills, particularly those that no one has tended.

Their beauty is evident for all to see. We should have that natural beauty of our Creator emitting from our lives. God is most pleased with our character and our heart that shares His love and goodness, not focusing on the external things.

Are you focused on sharing the internal beauty of God in you with others?

ENJOY THE VIEW.

> *"Command those who are rich in this present world not to be arrogant nor to put their hope in wealth, which is so uncertain, but to put their hope in God, who richly provides us with everything for our enjoyment. Command them to do good, to be rich in good deeds, and to be generous and willing to share."*
> ~ 1 Timothy 6:17-18

Trees enjoy being trees. Do you need to be inspired to not compare yourself to other people and enjoy the life God has given you? We should take one day, one thing at a time, enjoying the people and blessings God gives us. We are encouraged to enjoy the view of God at work in us, others, and all of creation. We have the privilege of doing good and being generous with our time and talents to bring glory to God.

What is the latest gift God has given you to enjoy as you put your hope in Him?

Be encouraged while viewing God's beautiful creation of the trees to…

> truly be proud of the way you are living.
> go out on a limb to share your faith.
> grow your roots deep in faith.
> focus on the inner beauty of your heart.
> enjoy the view while being generous in spirit.

Christine M. Fisher

REFLECTION:

Which characteristic of the tree mentioned above do you need to work on most?
What change can you make today to be more like a tree?

"The glory of Lebanon will come to you, the juniper, the fir and the cypress together, to adorn my sanctuary; and I will glorify the place for my feet."
~ Isaiah 60:13

Section 2

GOD'S GLORY MANIFESTED IN PEOPLE

"I will say to the north and south, 'Bring my sons and daughters back to Israel from the distant corners of the earth. Bring all who claim me as their God, for I have made them for my glory. It was I who created them.'"
~ Isaiah 43:6-7 (NLT)

It is such an honor and privilege to know that out of all creation, God made us, yes, you and me, as His most special creation. God made us in His own image, which no other creation can say. God also gave us dominion over all creation.

Our lives should give glory to God with all we do and with all we are. We have the ability to manifest God's presence through our interactions and the way we love others and His creation. May we always glorify Him with our lives.

God's glory manifested in people.

"The glory of God is the human person fully alive."
~ St. Irenaeus

30

Amazing Things

"Publish his glorious deeds among the nations.
Tell everyone about the amazing things he does."
~ 1 Chronicles 16:24 (NLT)

In 2024, my website, hopetoinspireyou.com celebrated its tenth year of publishing weekly reflections. The first reflection posted titled, "An Unexpected Phone Call," was shared as a test to see if God would provide weekly inspiration for this endeavor.

"Ask and it will be given to you; seek and you will find; knock and the
door will be opened to you. For everyone who asks receives; the one who
seeks finds; and to the one who knocks, the door will be opened."
~ Matthew 7:7-8

That test was a form of asking and seeking God, seeing if the door would open. God is good and faithful, keeping His promises. I see that reflected in each reflection.

My goal has always been to inspire others in their faith journey and share how I see God in the ordinary things of life. Sometimes, we think God is up in heaven, too busy for us, and isn't working in our lives. I believe God's presence is found on earth and in all people. He is always at work in our lives, even when we might not see or feel it.

"I can never escape from your Spirit! I can never get away from your
presence! If I go up to heaven, you are there; if I go down to the grave, you

are there. If I ride the wings of the morning, if I dwell by the farthest oceans,
even there your hand will guide me, and your strength will support me."
~ Psalm 139:7-10 (NLT)

God is with us through the good and the bad. Wherever we are and whatever we are doing, God is with us, guiding and strengthening us. At times, we may try to walk away from God, but He is faithful and waits patiently for us to return. He is with us in the ordinary moments of our days. Do you see Him orchestrating events and relationships in your life?

Setting a goal of writing weekly helps me keep my eyes open to see God all around me. Being aware of God and communing with Him regularly has grown my faith. The weekly reflections help me articulate my thoughts and experiences so I can process and better understand my faith. When I click the publish button each week, I pray it may help at least one person see something through a different lens or encourage their faith walk.

Writing is my ministry, enabling me to share my faith and God with others. How grateful I am to see how God has grown and expanded the ministry with the publishing of four 90-day devotionals. Publishing a book was never on my radar, but as God produces growth in our lives and ministries, His will prevails. Some of my faithful readers first planted the seed of possibly publishing a book, which God brought to fruition.

"For when one says, 'I follow Paul,' and another, 'I follow Apollos,' are
you not mere human beings? What, after all, is Apollos? And what is
Paul? Only servants, through whom you came to believe—as the Lord
has assigned to each his task. I planted the seed, Apollos watered it, but
God has been making it grow. So neither the one who plants nor the
one who waters is anything, but only God, who makes things grow."
~ 1 Corinthians 3:4-7

Christine M. Fisher

God provided growth in my ministry, from writing weekly on a website to publishing four books to help spread the good news to more people. He used the simple act of seeing a bulletin advertisement for a speaker at a church to inspire me to go solo to the event. The speaker, a lady from Texas, and I talked for a few minutes after, and I remember that she prayed over me for my ministry. Little did either of us know that fifteen months later, she would feel led to publish my first book. Only God, who makes things grow, could orchestrate that.

> *"Publish his glorious deeds among the nations.*
> *Tell everyone about the amazing things he does."*
> ~ 1 Chronicles 16:24 (NLT)

That Scripture holds special significance for me, as I discovered it while preparing the manuscript for my first book. Seeing the glorious things God does in our lives, it has become my heart's desire to tell everyone about those amazing things. I am in awe of Him. I want to share His goodness and shout it from the rooftops. It has enabled this originally insecure and introverted gal to become more outgoing, stepping out in faith many times to share one of her books with total strangers, especially at church. God has greatly increased my sense of family through this simple act. Strangers quickly become family—even spiritual brothers and sisters in the Lord—in a short amount of time. Having meaningful relationships with like-minded people has been the greatest blessing in my life. We can learn from each other, support one another, and be challenged by people's faith.

God has put many special people in my path on this journey. Some inspired me to start and build my own website. God has provided editors who have encouraged me through the years and a Biblical scholar who ensures the accuracy of my interpretations. Others have inspired reflections by their lives. And you, my faithful readers, are most valuable. You breathe life into my spirit with your faithful reading as well as your encouraging words and comments.

"I thank my God every time I remember you. In all my prayers for all of you, I always pray with joy because of your partnership in the gospel from the first day until now, being confident of this, that he who began a good work in you will carry it on to completion until the day of Christ Jesus."
~ Philippians 1:3-6

Be encouraged this week to…

> ask, seek, and knock.
> use the unique gifts God has given you to glorify Him.
> look for ways you can minister to others.

REFLECTION:

How do you best share the amazing things God does in your life?
What door has God opened in your life?

> *"Great is the Lord and most worthy of praise; his greatness no one can fathom. One generation commends your works to another; they tell of your mighty acts. They speak of the glorious splendor of your majesty—and I will meditate on your wonderful works."*
> ~ Psalm 145:3-5

Christine M. Fisher

31

Priorities

Do you find that life keeps you so busy or distracted that you barely have time to catch your breath?

Isn't it easy to see how doing things can take our time away from what we should focus on?

Despite all the earthly things we are involved in, what is most important to keep our focus on?

That we remember...

WHY WERE WE CREATED?

    To praise and give glory to our Creator.

> *"I will extol the Lord at all times; his praise will always be on my lips. I will glory in the Lord; let the afflicted hear and rejoice. Glorify the Lord with me; let us exalt his name together."*
> ~ Psalm 34:1-3

WHO IS REALLY IN CHARGE OF EVERYTHING?

    God, our Almighty, sovereign Lord.

> *"'I am the Alpha and the Omega—the beginning and the end,' says the Lord God. 'I am the one who is, who always was, and who is still to come—the Almighty One.'"*
> ~ Revelation 1:8 (NLT)

WHERE IS OUR REAL HOME?

In heaven.

"But our citizenship is in heaven. And we eagerly await a Savior from there, the Lord Jesus Christ, who, by the power that enables him to bring everything under his control, will transform our lowly bodies so that they will be like his glorious body."
~ Philippians 3:20-21

While doing the routine things like working to pay the bills, running errands, or sitting at a child's games, remember to stay connected to the source, God, by...

> praying for others and conversing with the Lord, which can be done anytime and everywhere.
>
> giving thanks to the Lord for things or people you are interacting with or that come to mind.
>
> listening to inspiring music.
>
> taking a minute to text or email someone to let them know you are thinking of them or praying for them.
>
> finding ways to bless those you are in contact with through your kindness, love, and compassion, no matter where you are and whatever you are doing.

Try not to let earthly things take over. Let us not lose our focus or let earthly things rule over us.

Don't think when you are out and about in the depths of busyness that you are far from the Lord or not able to commune with Him.

I encourage you to look for ways to further the kingdom, above all else, in everything you do.

Christine M. Fisher

REFLECTION:

What activity can you incorporate prayer into?

Which focus item above do you need to work on?

> *"What good is it for someone to gain the whole world, yet forfeit*
> *their soul? Or what can anyone give in exchange for their soul?*
> *If anyone is ashamed of me and my words in this adulterous*
> *and sinful generation, the Son of Man will be ashamed of them*
> *when he comes in his Father's glory with the holy angels."*
> ~ Mark 8:36-38

32

God's Purposes

"The Lord Almighty has sworn, 'Surely, as I have planned, so it will be, and as I have purposed, so it will happen.'"
~ Isaiah 14:24

God directs our steps and can use everything in our lives to further His purposes.

"Mordecai sent this reply to Esther: 'Don't think for a moment that because you're in the palace you will escape when all other Jews are killed. If you keep quiet at a time like this, deliverance and relief for the Jews will arise from some other place, but you and your relatives will die. Who knows if perhaps you were made queen for just such a time as this?' Then Esther sent this reply to Mordecai: 'Go and gather together all the Jews of Susa and fast for me. Do not eat or drink for three days, night or day. My maids and I will do the same. And then, though it is against the law, I will go in to see the king. If I must die, I must die.'"
~ Esther 4:13-16 (NLT)

King Xerxes chose Esther, who hid her Jewish ancestry, to be queen of Persia because of her exceptional beauty. Mordecai, Esther's uncle who looked after her, overheard an assassination plot to kill the king, which Esther relayed to him. Haman, a chief advisor to the king, was distraught when Mordecai would not bow down to him. He found out Mordecai was a Jew and plotted to exterminate the Jews.

Mordecai encouraged Esther to inform King Xerxes about Haman's plot, claiming that it could be the reason she was queen. Esther knew that in order to talk to the king, she needed an invitation; otherwise, she would face death if the king did not extend his scepter. She was willing to die while trying to save the Jews. Queen Esther did talk to the king without an invitation, and he did extend his scepter. As a result, King Xerxes had Haman executed, and the Jews were saved. Queen Esther fulfilled God's plan by being in the right place at the right time.

After attending a church service, I saw a lady I knew in passing, but not personally. She had inadvertently gone out of the church at the opposite exit from where her car was, so she was making her way back around. That is the point at which I ran into her. Upon seeing me, she paused for a minute and then asked if I would keep in prayer an intention that was heavy on her heart, stating she felt I was a prayerful person. I said, "Certainly!" She was able to share about the situation, and outside of my comfort zone, I felt led to pray with her right then. At the end, we embraced.

I was in awe as I reflected on how perfectly ordered both of our steps were that day, with the sequence of each event in our lives that led us to cross paths. I also thought about the way we got to know each other. In September 2019, I volunteered at a local ministry house, and she was the contact person for this organization. Because I met her at the ministry house, I recognized her at church. At one point, I mentioned I had published two books and she asked about buying one. A month later, she asked for the second one, and she couldn't wait to tell me she read it in a day and a half because she couldn't put it down. That day at church, with God's perfect orchestration, I was able to present her with my third book.

Had I had not pursued that ministry opportunity, though it wasn't right for me at the time, I would not have known this lady. I would not have the privilege, let alone the gift, of joining in prayer for her intention. It was part of God's plan for us to meet in 2019, and to be able to stand in prayer with her.

We can walk in faith, knowing God works things out for us, especially when we give up control of how we think things should be. God makes beautiful things happen as we surrender more and more.

Be encouraged as you see how God…

> directs your steps.
>
> presents opportunities for trusting in His timing.
>
> is accomplishing His purpose through you.
>
> is asking you to give up control.
>
> makes beauty out of your surrender.
>
> works good out of something that didn't work out like you expected.

REFLECTION:

What situation did you see God work out for His purposes?
What is something God put in your path that wasn't your plan?

> *"We do, however, speak a message of wisdom among the mature, but not the wisdom of this age or of the rulers of this age, who are coming to nothing. No, we declare God's wisdom, a mystery that has been hidden and that God destined for our glory before time began."*
> ~ 1 Corinthians 2:6-7

33

Restoration

What does restoration mean? Dictionary.com defines it as: "a return of something to a former, original, normal, or unimpaired condition." Restoration makes something new again, possibly even better than it was before.

We see in Scripture several stories about restoration. Sometimes the restoration is in physical ways in our body. Other times, our spirit is restored with joy or peace when it has been lacking. Restoration can occur with inanimate objects like our houses or within relationships.

My friend texted me and said, "I wanted to share a story about the 'on time' God whom we adore. Last week, I was praying for my relationship with my neighbor to be restored. She is a Christian woman who suddenly dropped out of my life. We used to pray together, and last week I was keenly feeling the lack of our prayer time together. I prayed that the Lord would grace me with a prayer partner or restore the relationship with this woman. I thought I had done something to turn her away from me, and I didn't understand what happened."

She continued, "Last Tuesday evening, she texted me after seven **years** of silence! Her text said, 'Hi neighbor, got time to talk tonight?' My joy was off the charts, and our misunderstanding was resolved through His grace. If I hadn't asked the Lord to make this right, I would still feel like I had done something wrong. We ended our conversation with plans to pray together."

What I found encouraging about this story was how the Spirit…

is always on time.
brings restoration.
provides.
works everything out for our good.

THE SPIRIT IS ALWAYS ON TIME.

Often times, isn't it the Spirit's time and not our time? How often do we think we have the perfect plan and timing for things only to find out it didn't work the way we thought? My friend prefaced her story by sharing how it was God's perfect timing.

> *"Yet I am confident I will see the Lord's goodness while I am here in the land of the living. Wait patiently for the Lord. Be brave and courageous. Yes, wait patiently for the Lord."*
> ~ Psalm 27:13-14 (NLT)

What a blessing to see the Lord's goodness in our daily lives. We wait patiently to see how the Holy Spirit works out events in our lives in perfect timing. We have confidence knowing that God wants the best for us and works out the best orchestrations for us. It gives us strength to grow in trust more and more.

THE SPIRIT BRINGS RESTORATION.

The Spirit is timely in our lives. My friend, after seven years of silence, felt strongly that something was missing or broken in her relationship with her neighbor. She was in tune with the Spirit, bringing it to prayer.

> *"For since our friendship with God was restored by the death of his Son while we were still his enemies, we will certainly be saved through the life of his Son. So now we can rejoice in our wonderful new relationship with God because our Lord Jesus Christ has made us friends of God."*
> ~ Romans 5:10-11 (NLT)

Christine M. Fisher

The greatest restoration in all of history is the salvation we have through Jesus Christ, God's Son. Our perfect relationship with God was broken through Adam and Eve's sin. In God's mercy, grace, and great love, He still wanted unity with us. This restoration of oneness with God was made possible when Jesus came to earth, suffered death, and was resurrected three days later. This is God's love at its finest.

The Spirit Provides.

My friend was feeling the void of having a prayerful Christian friend close by to pray with. She brought her concern to the Lord and asked Him for a prayer partner or to restore the relationship with her prior one. What a beautiful prayer, open to different options.

> *"Ask and it will be given to you; seek and you will find; knock and the door will be opened to you. For everyone who asks receives; the one who seeks finds; and to the one who knocks, the door will be opened."*
> ~ Matthew 7:7-8

When we ask in faith, in accordance with God's will, He will answer our prayers in the way that is best for us. We need to ask, seek, and knock as we share our hearts with the Lord. It is good to be honest with God, letting Him know our needs and concerns. The Spirit provides what we need, giving us what we are looking for as He opens doors in our lives. Our Father knows best. We get to walk in trust, knowing He is always with us.

The Spirit Works Everything Out for our Good.

I believe that the Spirit is always working out every step of our lives. Often, we are unaware of the details that orchestrate the His work.

"And we know that in all things God works for the good of those who love him, who have been called according to his purpose."
~ Romans 8:28

As we faithfully keep our focus on God, walking in His ways and loving Him with our whole hearts, we can be assured that everything is working out for our good. We have the freedom to let go of the control we think we have over our lives. There is freedom in knowing deep within that God is sovereign and is working everything out perfectly. We will still encounter both the good and the bad, but we have the assurance that it is for our best.

Be encouraged to…

> be grateful for the Spirit who is right on time.
> trust the Spirit, knowing His timing is perfect in all things.
> thank God for His loving plan of restoration by sending Jesus for your salvation.
> see what God is restoring and making even better in your faith journey.
> see what the Spirit provides when you ask, seek, and knock.
> pray to the Spirit for something that needs to be restored in your life.
> praise God for something you saw Him work out in your life.
> reflect on how the bad is working out for your best.

REFLECTION:

What has God restored in your life?
What situation would you like God to restore for you?

"Now, Lord, do it again! Restore us to our former glory! May streams of your refreshing flow over us until our dry hearts are drenched again."
~ Psalm 126:4 (TPT)

Christine M. Fisher

34

Spread A Little Kindness

How can we spread a little kindness every day for Christ?

When we do any act of kindness, we should do it freely, not counting the cost, and keeping in mind that our giving is unto the Lord. Jesus gave himself so freely for each one of us that shouldn't we, with His power, do the same?

To help us spread kindness, we need to forget about ourselves and our trials and make other people a priority. We also need to slow down in order to be aware of other people and their needs.

Think of how you can show some kindness toward the people God puts in your path each day—be it family, friends, coworkers, or even strangers. Spreading kindness shares in God's glory.

Your kindness might be…

> asking about a relative.
> calling a neighbor who is homebound.
> giving a young mother a break from her children.
> leaving a surprise note to brighten someone's day.
> defending someone who has been wronged.
> leaving money for someone in need.
> saying a sincere "Have a nice day" to the stressed cashier.

Every person we meet is an opportunity to spread Jesus' love through our kindness. We never know the circumstances or situations that someone is facing or experiencing. By spreading kindness, we may ease their problems without knowing it. We may not always feel like showing kindness, and it might not always be easy, but it certainly is a blessing knowing that it is exactly what the Lord would do and expects from us.

Jesus' life gave us examples of spreading kindness. It did not matter to Jesus whether the people were lowly or lofty. Jesus showed kindness by healing the ten lowly outcasts of leprosy and by acknowledging the rich Zacchaeus, who was in a tree trying to catch a glimpse of Jesus passing by.

In our reaching out to one another in Jesus' name, we follow in His footsteps, and our reward in heaven will be great.

REFLECTION:

What act of kindness have you received that touched you?
What surprising act of kindness have you given recently?

> *"You're kind and tenderhearted to those who don't deserve it and very patient with people who fail you. Your love is like a flooding river overflowing its banks with kindness. God, everyone sees your goodness, for your tender love is blended into everything you do. Everything you have made will praise you, fulfilling its purpose. And all your godly ones will be found bowing before you. They will tell the world of the lavish splendor of your kingdom and preach out about your limitless power. They will demonstrate for all to see your miracles of might and reveal the glorious majesty of your kingdom."*
> ~ Psalm 145:8-12 (TPT)

35

The Simple Things

I revel in the simple, insignificant things that God uses for His glory. He uses everything for His glory. I pray these thoughts inspire you to see that happening in your life. Seeing this goodness, I believe, helps us to see our purpose of glorifying God with every activity and interaction we have.

I try to show my appreciation to people who encourage my faith journey or lead certain ministries that enrich me. Sometimes it's just a feeling that I should send a quick text to someone saying, "I'm praying for you," or send a picture of a meaningful screenshot.

I am a newer member of a Christian community that has encouraged my faith journey. Recently, I texted the man in charge to express my appreciation and decided to include a screenshot of a prayer that holds special meaning to me because, as a young teen, I typed this prayer and had it in a collection of inspirational writings.

I Said A Prayer For You Today

I said a prayer for you today
And know God must have heard.
I felt the answer in my heart
Although He spoke no word!

I didn't ask for wealth or fame
(I knew you wouldn't mind).
I asked him to send treasures
Of a far more lasting kind!

I asked that He be near you
At the start of each new day;
To grant you health and blessings
And friends to share your way!

I asked for happiness for you
In all things great and small.
But it was for His loving care
I prayed the most of all!

I also sent it to a few more people. It is a blessing to see how God can use something simple in different ways in people's lives. One friend, whom I've known for almost twenty-seven years, said, "Thank you, Christine. I'm familiar with this prayer and have shared it with others, just like you did with me. This is the first time, however, anyone has sent me this prayer, and I must tell you, it had a very powerful emotional impact on me. Tears are still running down my face." She then asked if we could meet for a meal sometime, as she wanted spiritual guidance.

With God's perfect orchestration, three hours later we were at a park enjoying lunch and fellowship. It was an unexpected encounter that came about because of a simple prayer. Much to our surprise, five hours passed as we talked, listened, laughed, cried, and prayed together. It was a special time seeing Jesus' face in someone who needed encouragement. At the end, she said, "This is just what the doctor would have ordered."

What stood out to me about these events?

The importance of…

following the inkling to spread good cheer.
connecting with others.

thinking, praying for, and communicating with
others throughout the day.

reaching out when we need a human voice to encourage us.
sharing our faith and faith journey with others.
relationships over our never-ending to-do list.

listening with our hearts and ears.
letting people know they are not alone.
praying with and for people.

"Therefore, whenever we have the opportunity, we should do
good to everyone—especially to those in the family of faith."
~ Galatians 6:10 (NLT)

In the different circumstances of our busy lives, can you try to take time to
see what good you can do? Can you hold the door open for the next person,
offer a "Have a good day" greeting, or let a car out of a busy intersection?

"And let us not neglect our meeting together, as some
people do, but encourage one another, especially now
that the day of his return is drawing near."
~ Hebrews 10:25 (NLT)

Can you find a few minutes to connect with a friend over coffee or take
a quick walk? It might just be enough to encourage the person and make
them smile.

"Understand this, my dear brothers and sisters: You must all
be quick to listen, slow to speak, and slow to get angry."
~ James 1:19 (NLT)

Do you need to practice listening with your heart? Try to truly listen with
your heart and ears rather than interrupting to share your own experience.

Be encouraged to…

spread a little extra goodness in the world.
take time to connect in person with someone.
listen with your heart to someone who is struggling.

Take a moment to reread the prayer and know that it is my prayer for you, my dear reader. God bless.

REFLECTION:

What is something you thought was insignificant that God used for His greater glory?
Who do you know that needs your listening heart?

> *"He will give eternal life to those who keep on doing good, seeking after the glory and honor and immortality that God offers."*
> ~ Romans 2:7 (NLT)

36

Hidden Treasures

Do you often think you are in charge of the events in your life? Truthfully, I like to think I am in control of things, but more and more, I realize and see God's orchestrations in my life. When I see the beauty of something that happens, I am in awe of seeing God's divine goodness in the many little steps that led to that point.

A case in point was being in the perfect spot getting out of the passenger side of the car to see a hidden treasure, which was a leaf in the shape of a heart sticking out amidst the blades of grass in our lawn. It started with planning a get-together with a few people to celebrate the newlyweds, aka my youngest son and daughter-in-love, who were home visiting after their honeymoon. Some unexpected events led us to eat at a different restaurant than I planned, which led to the timing to see the heart.

> *"I will give you hidden treasures, riches stored in secret*
> *places, so that you may know that I am the Lord, the*
> *God of Israel, who summons you by name."*
> ~ Isaiah 45:3

The Lord was speaking to King Cyrus, assuring him that He was working everything out for him to be victorious. God was with and in control of Cyrus' activities. He had a special plan for King Cyrus. God calls each of us by name, too, giving us hidden treasures in our lives because of His great love for us.

> *"The kingdom of heaven is like treasure hidden in a field, which*
> *a man found and covered up. Then in his joy he goes and sells all*
> *that he has and buys that field. Again, the kingdom of heaven is*

like a merchant in search of fine pearls, who, on finding one pearl
of great value, went and sold all that he had and bought it."
~ Matthew 13:44-46 (ESV)

What is the kingdom of heaven like? Scripture tells us it is like the joy we feel when we find a hidden treasure in a field or a valuable pearl. We go to any length to obtain the treasure because we are excited to find it. My spirit was filled with joy when I saw the hidden heart-shaped treasure as I experienced the kingdom of heaven on earth. What an awesome God we have who is always speaking to us.

May you see the beauty and awesome power of God as He reveals His hidden treasures in your life. Try to be more aware of all the circumstances of your life, as God works everything out for you. God's plans are not always ours, but we can trust that they are always the best, even when life is difficult.

Be encouraged to…

> surrender control to God and see Him work everything out according to His will.
> see what hidden treasures God brings into your life.
> experience true joy when unexpected treasures appear.

REFLECTION:

What is the latest hidden treasure that God provided for you?
Are you overcome with joy when you find the hidden treasures of love from God?

"For God, who said, 'Let light shine out of darkness,' made his
light shine in our hearts to give us the light of the knowledge
of God's glory displayed in the face of Christ."
~ 2 Corinthians 4:6

Christine M. Fisher

37

Rise Above

Do you get stuck dwelling on the negative circumstances happening in your life?

Do you know anyone who seems, despite difficult circumstances, to rise above those things and shine their light to bless others?

Are you inspired to emulate how you see them living?

I find these people most inspiring. My faith walk was encouraged by visiting a dear friend, Greg, who was recovering from hip replacement surgery. Decades earlier, Greg had surgery to remove a tumor at the base of his brain inside the spinal cord, which left him with physical limitations. Because of this, his recovery from hip replacement surgery was even more difficult and involved. These visits provided me with a two-fold message.

This was my first time visiting a VA hospital which I consider an honor and a holy place. As I went through the revolving doors, the first thing I noticed was a sign that said,

> *"To care for him who shall have borne the battle,*
> *and for his widow and his orphans."*
> ~ Abraham Lincoln

I was overwhelmed with the thought that all the people in this hospital had served in the military in some capacity. They were now battling wars of their own, most likely because of their time serving our country. I saw one gentleman with no legs lying in bed. Many were in wheelchairs. Oh, the stories each individual could share about fighting to keep our nation free. I thought about the many sacrifices the veterans and their families must have endured, battling different issues, both while they served and in the years after.

This particular facility was very impressive. The one day I visited was warm and sunny, so Greg was at the therapy terrace, which is a place they can go for physical therapy. It allows them to get fresh air and see a view of the city. The terrace also has picnic tables, vegetable garden containers, and a few games for the patients and their families to play. Special meals are also served there, and the veterans can be seen helping in whatever capacity they can. Throughout the week, groups of people like the Ladies Auxiliary, various VFW organizations, and even church groups take special meals to the veterans to give them a change in their regular dietary food. A couple in their 80s, the husband having served in the Marines, arrives every single day to play a guitar and sing to the residents. How special is that?

People are Willing to Rise Above their Personal Circumstances to Minister to Others in their Time of Need.

Greg was scheduled to be in physical therapy for another hour the first day I went to visit him, so I traced my steps back to the car to get my Bible and book. I saw a sign to the chapel, so I stopped there to pray, read, and wait for Greg to return. It was special to pray for and think about the people in the facility, as well as for the caregivers for these veterans. A few tears came to my eyes.

When I made my way back to Greg's room, he had a visitor, a man in a wheelchair, who came to visit him. This gentleman has been in a wheelchair for about three years, but he has also risen above his circumstances. He plans on participating in a twenty-six mile wheelchair race, so he faithfully trains every day, doing three-hour rides, with the goal of riding fourteen miles every day until the big race. That particular day, his plan was to ride for seven miles.

WHAT A WAY TO RISE ABOVE CIRCUMSTANCES.

Greg is always such a pleasure to visit. Despite being in pain twenty-four hours a day and unable to walk, he remains positive, asking questions, sharing prayer concerns for others, and making others feel loved. Greg shared about some of the different people there, some who had been there for three months or longer. Despite the pain and suffering, and even having to be hoisted out of bed with a special apparatus, Greg could be seen visiting other people, bringing the light of Christ to them. I see Greg's life giving glory to God.

WHAT A WAY TO RISE ABOVE THE NEGATIVE CIRCUMSTANCES HE IS DEALING WITH! WHAT A WONDERFUL EXAMPLE FOR US ALL TO KEEP IN MIND.

As I visited Greg, I could tell he was in great pain. His body was spasming because of the pain he was experiencing from his recent surgery. To keep his hips and legs from coming together, and to allow proper healing, he had to have a foam contraption between his legs for a period of six to eight weeks. I could not help but shed tears that day. Praying with him was the natural thing to do. As I left, Greg said something to the effect of, "God has a reason for me being here. We have to just keep going."

I am happy to report that two weeks after his hip replacement surgery, he was able to stand up and walk four feet, which was to see what specific areas he needs to focus on in physical therapy to progress even further. His next stop will be moving to a local sub-acute care rehab facility before heading back home. We continue to pray that Greg will be in even better physical shape than before the surgery, enabling him to walk short distances, most likely with a walker.

I encourage you to do two things:

Find a way to thank a veteran and/or their family for their sacrifices. You can do this verbally or by sending a card.

Rise above the negative circumstances you might be experiencing and reach out to someone in need. Maybe you can visit someone in a nursing home or pray for those who are suffering.

REFLECTION:

Who has impacted your life by the way they rise above their circumstances? Is there a veteran you can thank for their service?

> *"Now if we are children, then we are heirs—heirs of God and co-heirs with Christ, if indeed we share in his sufferings in order that we may also share in his glory. I consider that our present sufferings are not worth comparing with the glory that will be revealed in us."*
> ~ Romans 8:17-18

38

Moment by Moment

Lord, help us to take
One day at a time
Not worrying about tomorrow
And live **moment by moment.**

Help us live each day
To the fullest for your glory
Soaking in the richness of everything
And live **moment by moment.**

Lord, help us to see
You in everything around us
How you work mightily
While we live **moment by moment**.

Lord, help us to continually
Be refreshed
And renewed by your presence
As we live each moment
Moment by moment for you!

REFLECTION:

How well do you live moment by moment?
Do you recognize that each moment you live is for God's glory?

"And my God will meet all your needs according to the riches of his glory
in Christ Jesus. To our God and Father be glory for ever and ever. Amen."
~ Philippians 4:19-20

39

Graduation

It was a bit sentimental attending my youngest son's college graduation and soaking up the excitement of everyone there. He was my only child who opted to attend his college graduation, so my heart was filled with joy at sharing in the experience. It was a special bonus that we unknowingly sat at the end of an aisle that was exactly where he processed. As the graduates began the procession, my thoughts turned to the similarities between our faith journeys and the time when we are called to graduate from this earth and are ushered into heaven.

EXCITEMENT AND JOY IN LOOKING FOR THEIR LOVED ONES WHO SHARED IN THIS MILESTONE.

> *"Then Jesus told them this parable: 'Suppose one of you has a hundred sheep and loses one of them. Doesn't he leave the ninety-nine in the open country and go after the lost sheep until he finds it? And when he finds it, he joyfully puts it on his shoulders and goes home. Then he calls his friends and neighbors together and says, "Rejoice with me; I have found my lost sheep." I tell you that in the same way there will be more rejoicing in heaven over one sinner who repents than over ninety-nine righteous persons who do not need to repent.'"*
> ~ Luke 15:3-7

What excitement and joy there is in heaven whenever someone comes to the point of repenting from their old ways because they accept Jesus as their Savior. They are brought into the sheepfold of Jesus, the Good Shepherd.

Christine M. Fisher

As the graduates were processing in, they were looking around, hoping to spot their loved ones. Some were smiling and beaming in excitement, waving to their family and friends. Others looked a bit sad or anxious if they could not find the familiar faces they were looking for. When the graduates walked the stage as their names were called, a few shouts of "She's my sister" or "He's my brother" could be heard. People wanted them to know how much they were loved and that their family was proud of what they had accomplished.

The Importance of People who Played a Special Role in Their Lives.

"So Joshua fought the Amalekites as Moses had ordered, and Moses, Aaron and Hur went to the top of the hill. As long as Moses held up his hands, the Israelites were winning, but whenever he lowered his hands, the Amalekites were winning. When Moses' hands grew tired, they took a stone and put it under him and he sat on it. Aaron and Hur held his hands up—one on one side, one on the other—so that his hands remained steady till sunset."
~ Exodus 17:10-12

Who would think that holding up someone's hands would be a special role? Aaron and Hur filled that role so that Moses was able to endure a whole day holding the staff of God, and because of it, God kept the Israelites safe, allowing Joshua to defeat the Amalekites.

Before the ceremony began, there were touching videos of different graduates who thanked their parents, family, friends, mentors, and professors along their journey. The few students who gave speeches did likewise. All of the people that were mentioned helped give the emotional or physical support that was needed to persevere and make it through successfully. They shared in the struggles and the victories, giving encouragement to overcome obstacles.

HARD WORK PAYS OFF.

"Whatever you do, work at it with all your heart, as working for the Lord, not for human masters, since you know that you will receive an inheritance from the Lord as a reward. It is the Lord Christ you are serving."
~ Colossians 3:23-24

We should all work with our whole hearts on whatever we are doing. All that we do, from running a simple errand to giving a speech at a notorious college, should be done unto the Lord. We are ultimately serving Christ in all we do and sharing in His love. He rewards the attitude of our hearts.

The videos also showcased the hard work the students had put into their studies to be successful. Hours of reading, studying for tests, and doing projects or student teaching took place to be successful in obtaining their respective degrees. The graduates spent countless hours dedicating themselves to studying so they could become better people and provide for themselves and their families. Several students were juggling raising families and working different jobs while attending college.

May these graduates inspire us to continue running the race of life with excitement and joy while walking in faith, not fear.

May we live each day with a sense of accomplishment as we love and serve those in our path. I pray we may motivate each other to do good works as we strive together to be better reflections of Jesus. And when we are ushered into heaven, we will hear, "Well done, good and faithful servant!"

Be encouraged to...

> share in someone's excitement and joy at achieving a milestone.
> thank someone specifically for the way they have played a major role in your life.
> put everything into all you do to bring glory to God.

REFLECTION:

Who is someone you can thank today for the special role they played in your life?

Do you live by giving your all to God in everything?

> *"When the Son of Man comes in his glory, and all the angels with him, he will sit on his glorious throne. All the nations will be gathered before him, and he will separate the people one from another as a shepherd separates the sheep from the goats."*
> ~ Matthew 25:31-32

40

A Time of Refreshment

What constitutes a time of refreshment for you?

One of my definitions of refreshment is a retreat center, best described as…

> time at a peaceful, beautiful holy place on a lake.
> a peaceful, scenic drive soaking in God's wondrous creation.
> a simple room with just a bed and a small desk, chair, and sink.
> no other commitments.
> quiet time alone.
> serving and loving others as Christ did.

Do you have a group of people you consider family, even though you do not share the same DNA?

I experienced that special family bonding while working at the retreat center. When I left, I felt that the people had become family. Hugs and love were shared with one another as we departed. God softened my heart and helped me love the way He does through that weekend. This was the first time I worked alongside a woman from my own church and a special friend, which added to the family atmosphere.

Each time I serve at this retreat center, it seems like a special thought or experience presents itself. This time was no different. Being beside the lake and the beautiful hills refreshes my soul and spirit, especially when soaking in God's beautiful creation in the summer.

Christine M. Fisher

I am always in my element on these extended weekends because I am there to help set up the dining room for meals and prepare snacks throughout the day. I feel empowered when I am able to help others, see a need, and fill it. Paying attention to detail, jumping in when I hear of someone needing something, and reviewing things are always challenges I am ready to tackle.

Much planning goes into making sure things work together smoothly to get as perfect an outcome as can be achieved. We spent much time perfecting the science of each meal by having a big chart or checklist for each meal where everything is laid out: what goes on each table, what is refilled each meal, and what dishes are needed so that anyone can look at the list, fill the need, and then mark it off. We strive to get every item on the table in the exact spot on each of the tables. People feel loved when small details like these are not overlooked.

I was refreshed by…

> taking time to care for coworkers who were having a rough day.
> stretching myself by saying "yes" to doing a Scripture reading.
> trying to receive words of affirmation with grace and humility.
> being able to joke around with the kitchen staff and others to create happiness and joy.
> having a lady look to me when she felt anxious because of my calming spirit.
> working as a team to accomplish a goal.

Throughout the three days, we all bonded, shared many laughs, shared the ups and downs of issues people were experiencing, and worked together to plan and execute the meals seamlessly.

It was a wonderful time of blessing others, growth within me in different areas, great teamwork, and fun. My life has been enriched by meeting more beautiful people while filling a simple need. It just goes to prove that you never know how God will use your simple "yes" to bless others and refresh you at the same time.

REFLECTION:

What constitutes a time of refreshment for you?
What special family are you a part of?

> *"To the elders among you, I appeal as a fellow elder and a witness of Christ's sufferings who also will share in the glory to be revealed: Be shepherds of God's flock that is under your care, watching over them— not because you must, but because you are willing, as God wants you to be; not pursuing dishonest gain, but eager to serve; not lording it over those entrusted to you, but being examples to the flock."*
> ~ 1 Peter 5:1-3

41

Your Words are Influential

Have you reflected on the influence your words have on others?

Your words have the ability to build others up or tear them down.

One weekend, I was trying to decide whether to go to a family reunion, five hours away, or stay home. The first night of the reunion, when I was still home, my sister-in-law jokingly called and asked what toppings I wanted on the pizza they were ordering. It made me smile that she thought of me and called, asking if I was coming the next day. Because I was overwhelmed with pressing deadlines from work and nursing two of my kids who had their wisdom teeth out, I told her I would decide the next morning.

The next morning, my sister-in-law texted to say she thought I should come, letting me know she wanted me there to join in the festivities. Her words inspired me to say "yes." I would be taking the trip alone, so I started packing and soon was on the road. Though it was supposed to rain along the way, it never did. I listened to music and didn't have any traffic delays. I am thankful I went, and everyone seemed happy to see me.

At times, our words can have an adverse effect on a person.

Can you think of a time when someone said something to you that was cutting and hurtful?

Maybe the comments made you feel incompetent in some area of your life.

In many cases, it is likely the person did not realize their comment hurt you. In this case, you can choose to alienate yourself from the person, tell them how you feel, or choose to forgive them and move on.

Remember, your words have the power to build someone up or tear them down. Try to think before you speak in the hopes of encouraging others along their journey and use your words to give glory to God. A simple statement or two can have a big influence on how someone views themselves or a situation.

REFLECTION:

Do you need to forgive someone for their words that hurt your spirit? When was the last time someone spoke influential words that changed your life?

> *"Blessed are those who have learned to acclaim you, who walk*
> *in the light of your presence, Lord. They rejoice in your name*
> *all day long; they celebrate your righteousness. For you are their*
> *glory and strength, and by your favor you exalt our horn."*
> ~ Psalm 89:15-17

42

Strength In Unity

An important theme that resonated in my life recently was one of unity and how there is strength in unity. It started at church on the weekend, where I felt oneness with the Lord as He embraced me in His loving arms. I experienced God saying I am loved just as I am, despite my flaws and failings.

A friend, via text, shared some heartache a relative was going through. I encouraged him and was proud to see how he tried to battle his negative thoughts. At one point, he said, "I just reached out my hand to hold yours." My response was,

"What an honor...
Hold on tight...
We journey together.
Together is better...
There is more strength."

Even though we were communicating via text, I felt a spiritual connection with God and my friend. We were united in Spirit, and strength was a by-product.

I knew it would be a harder day for another friend on the two year anniversary of his mother's admittance to heaven. They had been close, and he devoted much time to caring for her when she was ill. Again, via text, I let my friend know that I was journeying with him as he remembered her that day, sharing that he continues her legacy. Through our text exchanges, I felt a unity with the Spirit and this friend.

Reflecting on the unity of the Spirit, I thought about this Scripture story:

"They devoted themselves to the apostles' teaching and to fellowship, to the breaking of bread and to prayer. Everyone was filled with awe at the many wonders and signs performed by the apostles. All the believers were together and had everything in common. They sold property and possessions to give to anyone who had need. Every day they continued to meet together in the temple courts. They broke bread in their homes and ate together with glad and sincere hearts, praising God and enjoying the favor of all the people. And the Lord added to their number daily those who were being saved."
~ Acts 2:42-47

This beautiful Scripture is how life should be lived, giving a glimpse into life in the church after Jesus' ascension into heaven. The apostles had just received the Holy Spirit and were in unity with the Spirit, one another, and all the believers who were considered a part of the church. Isn't it wonderful to see how they took care of each other's physical and spiritual needs? Everything they had was shared, so no one was in need. Their hearts were sincere in looking out for each other, and they praised God as one. When we are united in the Spirit and with one another, we receive strength.

Be encouraged to…

> be united with the Spirit.
> see what ways you can have spiritual unity with others.
> experience the by-product of the strength the Spirit provides.
>
> reach out your hand to grasp the hand of someone in need.
> journey with someone who is struggling.
> share the strength gained from being united with others.

Christine M. Fisher

REFLECTION:

How can you spur someone on to have a closer relationship with Jesus? What spiritual food can you offer someone in need?

> *"I pray that they will all be one, just as you and I are one—as you are in me, Father, and I am in you. And may they be in us so that the world will believe you sent me. 'I have given them the glory you gave me, so they may be one as we are one. I am in them and you are in me. May they experience such perfect unity that the world will know that you sent me and that you love them as much as you love me.'"*
> ~ John 17:21-23 (NLT)

43

God's Orchestrations

One day I saw a Facebook ad about an upcoming women's retreat. I did not know the speaker or worship leader, but I'm always game for a new adventure and learning more about our great God. Despite the short notice, when I emailed inquiring if there was availability, there was. God's orchestration. Off I went, solo for the weekend.

The event started with a buffet dinner. As I was in line, I asked the Lord to give me the courage to show myself as friendly. There were 320 women in attendance, and I believe I was the only one who attended alone. I sat at a table with older ladies who were also quiet, so it was a bit awkward.

After dinner, we went to the first session and then returned to the dining area for a coffeehouse concert. I sat with three ladies who were part of a larger group. Two other ladies from the same church sat with us. God's orchestration. The ladies were friendly and interesting to talk with. Many smiles and laughs were exchanged that evening.

Eventually, there was only one lady and me left at the table. It was a special encounter being two strangers sharing our stories as we encouraged, listened, and learned from each other. We were the last people to leave. It is always a blessing to make new friends.

Out of 320 ladies, how was it that the next morning, one lady of the three saw me at the buffet line and invited me to sit with them? God's orchestration. This happened again and again. We would be walking from two different places, and our paths would cross.

At lunch, I sat with the lady from the coffeehouse and others from her church. One of the ladies was talking about the ziplining she did the previous year. I was contemplating whether to try ziplining at this retreat, but it was only available for an hour and a half, and I already had a massage scheduled.

I left the cafeteria and headed to check out the zipline when my path crossed with the three ladies who invited me to go on a hayride with them. God's orchestration. A sense of relief swept over me, as I really didn't want to do the zipline. By the time the hayride returned, it wouldn't leave me enough time before the massage. When I arrived fifteen minutes early for the massage, I was told by the therapist that my appointment had been scheduled for earlier in the day. I began to think that maybe I was supposed to go ziplining since the massage time had gotten mixed up.

The ziplines were done in tandem, and there was one lone gal there, last in line. Once again, it was God's orchestration that I came along so we each had a partner to go with. She had never ziplined, and we were both scared while trying to have faith that everything would be okay. Getting to the zipline was easy because there was no high climb. We only had five stairs made of railroad ties and then a short walk through the woods. Being on the runway at the beginning of the platform still made me nervous, and my hands were sweaty. But it felt good to conquer another zipline.

During our free time, I bumped into the main speaker. This was another example of God's orchestration, as I wanted to thank her and share something with her.

It was delightful to close out the retreat by sitting with the three gals for lunch before we departed. The laughs we shared will always be dear to my heart. God's orchestration blesses me. As we exchanged hugs and good-byes, I was blessed that one lady even called me sweetheart a few times.

As I neared the last few streets before returning home, God's orchestration provided one last smile for me. The song *Show Me Your Glory* by my favorite band, Third Day, came on the radio. So often, God blesses me with hearing a Third Day song in my travels, even short ones, reminding me of His presence.

Do you, like me, often feel like **you** are in charge of things in your life, even the different decisions you make in a day? There was something about that weekend where my eyes were opened even more to see that God's orchestration is so very real. It was a reminder that **He** truly is in control of everything in **my** life.

I marvel at God's perfect orchestration of events in our lives, though it comes as no surprise to me. I am in awe of His presence and can't help but continue to share those things to bring glory to God, along with the hope that others will see Him working in their lives too.

What should I fear if He is orchestrating everything for me?

I pray you may be encouraged to see God's orchestration in your life.
Be reminded that He truly is in control of everything.
What should you fear if He is orchestrating everything for you?

REFLECTION:

What was the last perfect orchestration you saw in your life?
Do you trust God to work everything out for you?

> *"But we ought always to thank God for you, brothers and sisters*
> *loved by the Lord, because God chose you as firstfruits to be*
> *saved through the sanctifying work of the Spirit and through*
> *belief in the truth. He called you to this through our gospel, that*
> *you might share in the glory of our Lord Jesus Christ."*
> ~ 2 Thessalonians 2:13-14

Christine M. Fisher

44

The Cheerleaders

I try to challenge myself to do new and different things. This helps me grow, expands my horizons, and builds my confidence, knowing I am capable of doing things that at first may seem impossible. Having someone cheer me on is powerful and lends a little extra encouragement.

I survived riding a horse for the first time at Virginia Beach a few years ago, and the previous year, I rode a horse in the hills of Curacao, despite being scared. While at a Christian dude ranch, my friend mentioned she wanted to pet the horses. To challenge myself, I decided to help groom the horses.

The wranglers were welcoming, and I arrived at the barn by 7 a.m. for a time of devotion and then grooming. I cleaned one side of the horses while a wrangler did the other side. It was a good way to get more comfortable with the beautiful creatures and to love them—something I haven't done before. I felt quite accomplished with experiencing five trail rides throughout the week. The wranglers were kind, helpful, encouraging, and even took me on a different path to make me feel more comfortable.

As I was finishing a trail ride one day, I walked to a pond where a fishing derby was taking place. A few guests were trying their hand at fishing, so I grabbed a pole, put the bait on it, and cast my line into the middle pond. I thought about casting all my cares and anxieties on God. Considering I hadn't fished since I was a kid, I was proud of my casting.

As I attempted to take a selfie of my fishing adventure, a staff member came to my rescue. Just as he came over, my pole started pulling, and I reeled in a fish. It was perfect timing as he helped me get the fish off the hook. The fish, measuring 11.6 inches, topped the prior record of 11.5 inches. I won the fishing derby, and my prize was a free ice cream sundae, with all the toppings.

In the horse arena area, the ranch offered the activity of using sling shots, knives, and hatchets to hit a target. With enough persistence and cheering from both guests and workers, I was eventually able to get all three weapons on the target, even one particularly heavy hatchet that was quite the challenge to throw. One lady guest at the ranch was so impressed that I was able to do them all, whenever I saw her, she would smile and mention my throwing skills.

On our last day, the rock wall and zipline were open. I was excited to do the zipline, especially since this one did not have a rough landing at the end. What I did not realize was that the only way to get to the beginning of the zipline was by climbing a very tall rock wall. I am afraid of heights. But I donned the rock wall gear and waited while some young children went first. Once making it to the top of the rock wall, one had to climb over the top and wait on the high platform before getting harnessed for the zipline.

I was there with a group of three ladies, one of whom was the lady impressed with my throwing skills, along with two mothers of children who were there. They, along with my friend, were proud that I was attempting this feat and encouraged me. As I was waiting, doubt crept into my mind. Seeing how tall the wall was and thinking about waiting on the platform, **if** I made it, produced more fear and sweaty hands. At last, it was my turn. When I asked the staffers if everyone made it up the rock wall, their reply was, "No, not everyone is able to do it."

There are two sections of the rock wall, and climbing with a person next to you is the norm. I attempted the route that was supposedly a little easier. I took a deep breath and stepped to the wall to begin my ascent. As I climbed, I was thirsty from the Colorado elevation, the hot climate that day, and I was weak from a horse ride I had taken right before arriving at the rock wall. Looking up, I felt like I was hyperventilating and doubted my ability. The staffer tried to tell me the way to go, but it was overwhelming, and I couldn't gain enough strength to move. So, I surrendered at that point. I came down, kept my gear on, and waited for a few ladies to go ahead of me.

There were about fifteen minutes left for the activity, and the clock was ticking. The ladies who went ahead of me were successful and encouraged me to try again as I had hydrated, and they were giving me pointers on being victorious. With less than five minutes remaining, I gave that rock wall one more valiant attempt. It was great to have so many ladies give words of encouragement and instructions on where to put my feet and hands. They kept saying, "You can do it; keep going; you've got this."

I did get further, about halfway up, before succumbing to the fact that I could not get all the way to the top. My arms and legs couldn't stretch far enough to continue. I am proud I gave it my best and, though I feel I am in the best shape currently, it was a little too difficult.

What touched me the most was the support and encouragement offered to me. What a wonderful thing to have others cheering you on during something difficult.

REFLECTION:

When were you a cheerleader, encouraging someone through a difficult task? Who cheered you on by giving you strength to do something you thought you couldn't?

"If anyone speaks, they should do so as one who speaks the very words of God. If anyone serves, they should do so with the strength God provides, so that in all things God may be praised through Jesus Christ. To him be the glory and the power for ever and ever. Amen."
~ 1 Peter 4:11

45

Precious Angel

This reflection is dedicated to all the parents who have lost a baby or child, no matter what age. These words come from Jesus' heart. May you be comforted by Him and others who care. These words are also fitting for anyone who has lost someone special.

Every life is so precious to Me
No matter how small the child
Even the tiniest baby, within its mother be,
Is a treasure and special angel in My plan.

I know every tear you've shed
Every dream you've dreamed
I hear every prayer that is said
And I know how much your heart aches.

Though many sacrifices and pain
You have endured
Know they were not in vain
They are steps that were part of My plan.

I know the burden is hard to bear
And the pain is great
But know that I care
And I bring you comfort.

Someday soon you will see
Your angel in My heavenly kingdom
But in the meantime, be
Assured that your angel is safe in My arms.

REFLECTION:

Can you stretch yourself to walk with another as they grieve through the years?

What has been the greatest comfort you have received in your loss?

> *"These trials will show that your faith is genuine. It is being tested*
> *as fire tests and purifies gold—though your faith is far more*
> *precious than mere gold. So when your faith remains strong through*
> *many trials, it will bring you much praise and glory and honor*
> *on the day when Jesus Christ is revealed to the whole world."*
> ~ 1 Peter 1:7 (NLT)

46

Value Opportunities

"Value the opportunities you're given. They will
affect more than you can see right now."
~ Melody Lavin

Every day, opportunities, both big and small, present themselves in our lives; we can either say "yes" or "no" to them, and we often don't know the impact of our response. Our answer can have a ripple effect, either immediately or years later, either in our personal lives or in the lives of others. Our decision can also impact the lives of those we don't know. That is the beauty of our faith and trust in the Lord, as we remind ourselves that He is always working everything out for our good. There is more to life than just our little world. We will learn more about the impact we have made on others when we are in heaven.

"When one of those at the table with him heard this, he said to
Jesus, 'Blessed is the one who will eat at the feast in the kingdom of
God.' Jesus replied: 'A certain man was preparing a great banquet
and invited many guests. At the time of the banquet he sent his
servant to tell those who had been invited, "Come, for everything
is now ready." But they all alike began to make excuses. The
first said, "I have just bought a field, and I must go and see it.
Please excuse me." Another said, "I have just bought five yoke of
oxen, and I'm on my way to try them out. Please excuse me." Still
another said, "I just got married, so I can't come." The servant
came back and reported this to his master. Then the owner of
the house became angry and ordered his servant, "Go out quickly

into the streets and alleys of the town and bring in the poor, the
crippled, the blind and the lame." "Sir," the servant said, "what
you ordered has been done, but there is still room." Then the master
told his servant, "Go out to the roads and country lanes and compel
them to come in, so that my house will be full. I tell you, not one
of those who were invited will get a taste of my banquet."""
~ Luke 14:15-24

This parable of the Great Banquet highlights the importance of taking advantage of opportunities that are put in our path every day. How many times do we, like those mentioned in this story, make excuses for not taking advantage of an opportunity? Maybe we are too tired to reach out to someone, we think we are too busy, or we put things above God. If we see God at work in our lives, bringing opportunities to us and taking advantage of them, we will live a more fulfilling life in union with the Spirit. Often, the opportunity might be something outside our normal comfort zone where God is stretching us for more growth.

Upon reflection, below are a few opportunities God has provided in my life:

THE OPPORTUNITY TO SHARE MY BOOKS WITH STRANGERS.

During the pandemic, I was grateful for the opportunity to work from home. Once the restrictions were lifted, I had more time and freedom to visit church. One day, I walked up to a stranger and handed him one of my books. Much to my surprise, two days later he emailed me, thanking me for the book and sharing his spiritual experiences.

The next day, we met after church to talk about the Holy Spirit and ministries in our lives. It was the beginning of a thirteen-month spiritual bond as we continued to share more. About six months after I met him, he found out he had cancer and he died six months later. I attended his funeral, which was out of town, and met his mother, sharing a book with her and explaining who I was. It is a blessing to keep in touch with her. She is a joy and has enjoyed the stories of her son I have shared.

I never dreamed that giving a book to a stranger would lead to a spiritual friendship and the ripple effect of meeting his mother. It has given her comfort knowing how her son's life and mine impacted each other as we shared our faith.

THE OPPORTUNITY TO SPEAK AT A LIBRARY.

A friend was scheduled to do some masterful storytelling at a public library but was unable to be present since he was in the hospital. He graciously thought it would be an opportunity for me to fill in and share about being a self-published author. When he first mentioned it, my initial thought was no; I could not do it, as I had to be conscious of different faiths and needed to talk in more general terms.

Much to my surprise, after asking a few people to pray for me and thinking of what I would share, I said "yes" to the opportunity. It was disappointing that only two people attended, my friend who is a faithful encourager of my writing journey, and the other who came to see the storyteller without realizing the schedule changed.

I proceeded with my talk, trusting that whoever was supposed to be there was. Both ladies were willing to share related personal stories, which is always a blessing. My friend felt led to purchase a book for the other person in attendance, so I trust that God will somehow encourage this lady in her faith journey with something I said or what she reads.

I never dreamed I would step out in faith to speak at a public library at the last minute. I knew it was important to trust that God had His reasons for only two people attending. It was most important for me to be obedient in this opportunity.

The Opportunity to Take Time to Visit with a Friend.

Relationships with people in our lives, particularly on this spiritual journey, are so important. God has provided more family for me through these friendships. I enjoy reaching out to people to keep connected.

Recently, one such friend and I went to breakfast at a place we had never been before. A few minutes after arriving, a couple that I know walked in and the wife said my friend looked familiar. After conversing, the wife realized she knew some of my friend's children, since she was an aide at their school when the children were little. A God moment.

On the way home, I told my friend how much growth I had seen in her faith, as she was growing stronger and more confident in looking at the bright side of even harder situations. We don't talk too often, so I was surprised when she shared that she feels a lot has to do with her reading my weekly reflections and books.

I never dreamed that taking advantage of an opportunity to visit with a friend would lead to us sharing how thankful we were for the other's presence in our faith journey. What a blessing to be reminded of the importance of our lives and the impact we have on each other.

Be encouraged to…

> value the opportunities that come your way.
> know your "yes" can have a greater impact than you can see.
> see the opportunities where you can be stretched in faith to step out of your comfort zone.
> make a list of the opportunities you see God giving you.

see if your answer is more "yes" or "no" to the opportunities that are presented to you.

create an opportunity to encourage someone.

REFLECTION:

What opportunity did God provide for you that was of great value?
Is there an opportunity you can extend to someone else to help them grow?

> *"In the same way, let your light shine before others, that they may see your good deeds and glorify your Father in heaven."*
> ~ Matthew 5:16

47

An 8-Minute Challenge

Do you feel that life is so busy you rarely have a few minutes to catch your breath?

It seems that when we are young adults and launching out on our own, we are busy making our mark and trying to have a successful career. Often, it takes extra hours to make a go of it. Many then settle into getting married and starting a family, which then becomes the top priority, along with juggling work and activities as the children grow.

Don't we always hear retirees say they don't know how they had time for anything when they were working? All that to say, it's easy to get so busy with activities and running places that we neglect what is most important, which is the value of relationships.

Despite the many pros of technology these days, like instant access to information and a form of connection with people, there are also many cons.

How many times do we see people walking around with their heads down, looking at their phones, too preoccupied to look up and say, "Hello?"

How about at restaurants where families or even two people are on their phones instead of talking to one another?

What if we strive to build relationships with people, specifically by talking to them in person or over the phone?

I recently received an email with the subject line "Hi and an 8-minute challenge" from a sister-in-law who lives in the state of Washington. Truth be told, being so far away from each other and our busy lives, we rarely take time to keep in touch.

She explained, "Over the holidays, the New York Times ran a set of articles in their Wellness section about staying in touch with family and friends and suggested making 8-minute phone calls as a way to do this even while we are all so busy. I thought it was an interesting idea, so I am checking in to see if you want to give it a whirl. The idea is that we would find an 8-minute slot each month to connect."

I thought it was a lovely idea, and four days later, we had our first 8-minute phone call that turned into 18 minutes. She alerted me when the eight minutes were up, and we decided to make it a little longer. It was life-giving to hear her voice and catch up.

"Let us think of ways to motivate one another to acts of love and good works. And let us not neglect our meeting together, as some people do, but encourage one another, especially now that the day of his return is drawing near."
~ Hebrews 10:24-25 (NLT)

This Scripture encourages us to connect with others through meeting together. If we are not physically able to meet with others because of distance or other circumstances, a phone call is the next best option. Talking versus text message or email lends itself to hearing the tone of voice and allows for a more concise conversation and better understanding. Knowing what lies behind the stories we hear allows us to better motivate and encourage one another. When we meet with others, it benefits us both and fresh life is breathed into both people.

Are you willing to consider a form of this challenge?
How about reaching out to just **one** person to test it out?

Christine M. Fisher

Can you think of one person you love—someone you miss or wish you connected with more often?

> Contact them to see if they would consider an 8-minute phone conversation or video chat, maybe once a month or whatever interval you decide on.

> Set a date and time for the first meeting, possibly sending them an electronic calendar invitation or marking your calendar the good, old-fashioned way.

We have the ability to brighten the day by connecting with others and letting them know they are loved. Think what a difference 8 minutes out of 1,440 in one day can make, even if only once a month.

Be encouraged to…

> make relationships a priority.
> reach out to one person for the 8-minute challenge.
> see how a short conversation can be heartfelt.
> share with someone how they have impacted your life.

REFLECTION:

Who did God bring to mind that you can contact?
Do you need to take time to focus more on relationships?

"For I want you to understand what really matters, so that you may live pure and blameless lives until the day of Christ's return. May you always be filled with the fruit of your salvation—the righteous character produced in your life by Jesus Christ—for this will bring much glory and praise to God."
~ Philippians 1:10-11 (NLT)

48

The Little Details

One Christmas, I thought my mother would appreciate a gift that was made in Jerusalem from an olive tree. I also decided to send her an angel ornament from the same company. When I was preparing the package to mail, I solicited the help of my youngest son, not telling him who the gift was going to. We had just sealed it when he said, "Oh, hold on." Noticing the little detail of who the package was for led him to go into his bedroom, grab some money and an envelope, and write a short message to his grandma. We stuffed his gift into the package and resealed it.

On Christmas Day, my mom called to say she enjoyed the gifts. When she opened the angel, she noticed there was a tag on it, placed there by the company, with the numbers 8/17 on it, which was the birthdate of her mom, my grandma, who died many years ago. What a little detail that only God could orchestrate.

My mom cried when she saw the thoughtfulness and kindness of my son in giving her some of his hard-earned money and the special note he wrote, encouraging her to spoil herself because she deserved it. She held back tears as she thanked him, saying she would keep the envelope, as it held special meaning for her.

During this holiday season, I was reminded of how God is always at work, even in the littlest of details in our lives. It is a never-ending ripple effect of His goodness and glory.

Christine M. Fisher

REFLECTION:

In what situation did you see God's hand at work in some little details? When did you surprise someone with a little detail that meant so much?

"A host always serves the best wine first,' he said. 'Then, when everyone has had a lot to drink, he brings out the less expensive wine. But you have kept the best until now!' This miraculous sign at Cana in Galilee was the first time Jesus revealed his glory. And his disciples believed in him."
~ John 2:10-11 (NLT)

49

Joyous Oneness

My second book, *God's Love Illuminated: Treasured Thoughts to Inspire Walking in God's Abundant Love*, received the Henri Award at the Christian Literary Awards in Arlington, Texas, on March 18, 2023, from Joy and Company in the category of Non-Fiction: Victorious Living. A panel of judges from different parts of the USA were given the task of reading books in a certain category and voting on the one they felt was most deserving of the award.

A friend said, "You must be so full of joy at receiving the award. It must have been a mountain experience."

As I thought about it, I said, "I'm not sure how much joy I feel specifically with the award. It was more like an acceptance of the honor at the time. I want to remain humble. I feel joy each week by writing for my website and being able to share God in the ordinary. It keeps me in oneness with the Lord."

She said, "It is okay to still feel that joy and to remain humble."

When they announced my name as the Henri Award recipient, I did not fear, which was a big step for me, nor was I overcome with emotion. It was like a peaceful acceptance of being in the moment. I had to quickly get my two-minute acceptance speech from my purse. I felt comfortable walking up on stage, taking the microphone out of its stand (it was too high for me), and starting my speech. About three quarters of the way through, I realized my legs were shaky, so I shared that with the audience just in case I fell over. I think I must have been in a little bit of shock. I stumbled over my words a little, but then God helped me regain my composure to finish my speech, receive the award, and exit the stage.

When I got back to my seat, I closed my eyes, folded my hands, and felt a oneness with the Lord. It is also what I experience at times in church. A time of just being, of the joy of being in His presence, of letting Him love me, and of a peace that reaffirms that I am on the path He has for me. If I can utter any words, it is just "thank you." My publisher leaned over and said, "Are you okay?" I responded, "Yes, I am just experiencing a oneness with the Lord."

The night was even more memorable with my publisher sitting next to me. It was only the second time we met face-to-face. The first time was when she was giving a talk at a church in my area in June 2019. Little did either of us know that she would feel the Lord calling her to be my publisher. She was also the one who encouraged me to submit my book to two literary contests after its publication in 2021.

My friend mentioned the passage about Jesus' transfiguration and wondered if it related to my experience receiving the Henri Award.

"After six days Jesus took with him Peter, James and John the brother of James, and led them up a high mountain by themselves. There he was transfigured before them. His face shone like the sun, and his clothes became as white as the light. Just then there appeared before them Moses and Elijah, talking with Jesus. Peter said to Jesus, 'Lord, it is good for us to be here. If you wish, I will put up three shelters—one for you, one for Moses and one for Elijah.' While he was still speaking, a bright cloud covered them, and a voice from the cloud said, 'This is my Son, whom I love; with him I am well pleased. Listen to him!' When the disciples heard this, they fell facedown to the ground, terrified. But Jesus came and touched them. 'Get up,' he said. 'Don't be afraid.' When they looked up, they saw no one except Jesus."
~ Matthew 17:1-8

Indeed, it does seem like the perfect description of what I encountered, especially when I returned to my seat. How wonderful it is to experience Jesus' presence at the different mountain times of our spiritual journey. Just as Peter wanted the time to never end, don't we feel that way too? Being immersed in oneness with Jesus transfigures our spirits. In my spirit, I was giving gratitude and thanksgiving to God for being able to share Him through the written word. He has opened so many doors, allowing me to grow and stretch for His glory. I have met so many people who quickly become spiritual friends and breathe life into my spirit and faith journey. I pray that I am doing everything He wants as I experience His love through His orchestrations. I hope He is well pleased. I am in awe of the ending of the above scripture where it says, *"Get up. Don't be afraid."*

Three days before this discussion with my friend, my publisher texted me. She shared an encouraging story of how she was asked to teach a Sunday school class where the Lord pointed out the words, *"Get up"* from Acts 9. She did some research and found the phrase in different stories in both the Old and New Testaments. In the New Testament, Jesus spoke the words often when He healed people. She personalized the message for me, saying, "Keep going, Christine. Keep getting up every morning and doing what Jesus says to do. You are right where He wants you!"

Seeing the words, *"Get up,"* in Matthew 17:1-8 is another confirmation. It's the third passage I have seen since she shared it with me. I believe the Lord is telling me personally to *"Get up. Don't be afraid."* I will continue to step out in faith and obedience.

This trip was the first time I visited Texas. My husband and I were able to sightsee in the Dallas and Fort Worth areas for two days, as well as take a tour of the AT&T Stadium, home of the Dallas Cowboys. My goal for the trip was to enjoy each moment and live in the present. I was pleasantly surprised to see that goal become a reality. From start to finish, I could not help but think what a gift the whole trip was. It was another beautiful ripple effect of this writing journey God has given me. I am so grateful and appreciate all the support and encouragement you, my friends and readers, have gifted me along the way.

Be encouraged to see how…

> Jesus transfigures your spirit.
> you hear God calling you His son or daughter and loving you.
> Jesus is calling you to *"Get up. Don't be afraid."*

REFLECTION:

What mountaintop experience have you had?
When have you felt a joyous oneness with the Lord?

> *"Publish his glorious deeds among the nations. Tell*
> *everyone about the amazing things he does."*
> ~ 1 Chronicles 16:24 (NLT)

50

Bucket List

Do you have a bucket list?

> If so, what types of things are on it?

Maybe to...

> take a trip overseas?
> retire early?
> go on a mission trip?
> run a marathon?

The only thing on my bucket list is to do a one-week mission trip. If it involved loving babies at an orphanage, that would be even better. On two different K-Love Christian Music cruises, God partially fulfilled that with the opportunity to assist on one-day mission trips.

What if we view it as God, rather than us, having a bucket list for our lives?

What if we consider some of the opportunities that come along for us as being on God's bucket list, even though they were never on ours?

"I make known the end from the beginning, from ancient times, what is still to come. I say, 'My purpose will stand, and I will do all that I please.'"
~ Isaiah 46:10

God is telling the people of Babylon and Israel that His purpose and plan to save and redeem them will prevail even when things look hopeless. God's perfect will reigns.

"Lord, I know that people's lives are not their own;
it is not for them to direct their steps."
~ Jeremiah 10:23

This verse is part of the prophet Jeremiah's prayer to God. Jeremiah knows that God directs people's steps and that our lives are ultimately God's.

"Many are the plans in a person's heart, but it
is the Lord's purpose that prevails."
~ Proverbs 19:21

Isn't it comforting to know that God's purpose prevails in our lives? His purpose for us may be different than the plans we make, but God knows what is best.

Different events over the last few years—things I never dreamed of—I see as God's bucket list for me. One event would be the privilege of taking a Holy Land pilgrimage. It was never anything I envisioned experiencing, but through joining a new church a few years earlier, God provided a pastor who was hosting a trip to the Holy Land.

As soon as I heard of it, I knew it was a bucket list item I wanted to pursue. Due to the pandemic, the trip was postponed a year, but it worked out perfectly in God's timing, and there were no lines at the sites, as we were the first tour group back in Israel after the pandemic. It was the trip of a lifetime that I will always treasure. Little did I know that God would lead me to have a section in my third devotional, *God's Compassion Illuminated*, published that same year, dedicated to sharing my pilgrimage experience.

Be encouraged to…

> view and live life through the lens of God's bucket list.
> see how God orchestrates the execution of His will for you.
> know God's bucket list is most important.

REFLECTIONS:

What event in your life do you see as God's bucket item for you?
What is an item on your bucket list?

> *"Give to the Lord the glory he deserves! Bring your offering and come*
> *into his presence. Worship the Lord in all his holy splendor."*
> ~ 1 Chronicles 16:29 (NLT)

51

The Blessing of People

These quotes have great truth and are worthy of taking a few minutes to reflect upon.

"We do not meet people by accident.
God places these people in our lives for a reason."

"Even if our time with someone expires, our prayers do not."

"Some people come into your life and challenge
you and change you for the better.
These are the people who you will always remember."

Do you notice those people God puts in your path, even with just a simple interaction, that blesses you in some way?

My friend and I were at a Christian concert and, before the concert began, we started conversing with the gentleman sitting next to us. I found out he is a writer, and I gave him a card about my website. It was interesting that a few of the things we were talking about before the concert were confirmed during the concert, as the singers were sharing. We both noticed it immediately—God at work making us smile. This gentleman's faith has been inspirational, as he comments on some of my weekly thoughts, providing me with great feedback and encouraging my writing.

At a women's retreat, a lady sat at my table for the last meal. We did not talk to each other at the retreat, but she asked for a card when she heard I had a website. She is the only person who has emailed me through my website, and I am blessed by getting to know her, the things she has been through, and sharing our love of the Lord and experiences.

As I try to walk through my neighborhood, God's perfect timing amazes me. It was perfect timing that I ran into a neighbor I used to know from church when I was growing up. She now lives in my neighborhood.

In the twenty or so years we have lived here, it is rare that we run into each other. This particular day, she was arriving home as I was walking near her house. She took a few minutes to ask about my family, and what my children were up to. Much to my surprise, she said she would be praying for my children. I was touched that a stranger felt led to pray for someone she doesn't know.

After the encounter, I remembered that I didn't think about sharing my website with her. I wrote her a quick thank-you note for offering to pray for my family and gave her my website information. God's still-small voice led me to put the note on her front door. As I was walking up the stairs, we caught each other by surprise. She was sitting at the far end of the porch, reading a book. It was a blessed encounter as we chatted about God and shared things in our lives. It was a simple, God-ordained moment that blessed me once again.

REFLECTION:

Who are some God-ordained people, significant in your faith journey, God has put in your path?
Who has helped challenge you to be a more Christ-like person?

> *"Save us, Lord our God, and gather us from the nations, that we may give thanks to your holy name and glory in your praise."*
> ~ Psalm 106:47

Christine M. Fisher

52

Living Well

"The purpose of life is not to be happy.
It is to be useful, to be honorable, to be compassionate,
to have it make some difference that you have lived and lived well."
~ Ralph Waldo Emerson

Have you wrestled with the meaning of life?

Why did God create you?

What is the purpose of your life?

Is there more to life than just the humdrum of daily routines?

THE PURPOSE OF LIFE IS NOT TO BE HAPPY.

At first glance, that line may seem disappointing, right? What if we interpret it more as meaning that being happy is not the most important thing or purpose of our lives? Isn't that a great truth?

Shouldn't the purpose of life be about being useful, honorable, and compassionate, knowing we make a difference in others' lives? I believe that constitutes a life lived well and gives God glory.

THE PURPOSE OF LIFE IS TO BE USEFUL.

"'Teacher, which is the greatest commandment in the Law?' Jesus replied:
'Love the Lord your God with all your heart and with all your soul
and with all your mind. This is the first and greatest commandment.
And the second is like it: Love your neighbor as yourself.'"
~ Matthew 22:36-39

What is the best way we can be useful while on this earth? I believe it is to follow the two greatest commandments of Jesus: to love God and our neighbor. We are most useful when we live a life of love. Sharing love will manifest itself through acts of service, truly caring for others, and showing them compassion.

The Purpose of Life is to be Honorable.

> "Do you not know that your bodies are temples of the Holy Spirit, who is in you, whom you have received from God? You are not your own; you were bought at a price. Therefore honor God with your bodies."
> ~ 1 Corinthians 6:19-20

The Holy Spirit lives in us, which makes our bodies temples of the Holy Spirit. What a privilege that is. We should make every attempt to live honorable lives to glorify God. From the way we treat our bodies with what we put into them physically, to the things we watch and fill our minds with, all should be honorable to God. Our actions in the way we live and how we treat others should also be honorable to God.

The Purpose of Life is to be Compassionate.

> "Praise be to the God and Father of our Lord Jesus Christ, the Father of compassion and the God of all comfort, who comforts us in all our troubles, so that we can comfort those in any trouble with the comfort we ourselves receive from God."
> ~ 2 Corinthians 1:3-4

God is to be praised for being the Father of compassion. His compassion comforts us, especially when we experience the most difficult of times. We are to live each day with the same compassion for those we encounter who are suffering and need comfort.

THE PURPOSE OF LIFE IS TO HAVE IT MAKE SOME DIFFERENCE THAT WE
HAVE LIVED WELL.

"Good friend, don't forget all I've taught you; take to heart my commands.
They'll help you live a long, long time, a long life lived full and well. Don't
lose your grip on Love and Loyalty. Tie them around your neck; carve
their initials on your heart. Earn a reputation for living well in God's
eyes and the eyes of the people. Trust God from the bottom of your heart;
don't try to figure out everything on your own. Listen for God's voice in
everything you do, everywhere you go; he's the one who will keep you on
track. Don't assume that you know it all. Run to God! Run from evil!
Your body will glow with health, your very bones will vibrate with life!
Honor God with everything you own; give him the first and the best."
~ Proverbs 3:1-9 (MSG)

How can we live and live well?

We need to take to heart God's commands, share His love, and be loyal.
We need to learn to trust Him more and more, knowing He works
everything out for our good.
We need to keep listening to and discerning God's voice and
leading in our lives, showing us what we should be doing.
We should flee from evil and run to God as we
honor Him with everything He has lavished us
with.

Be encouraged to see the various opportunities that arise to...

be useful by loving God above all else.
be useful in the ways you can love your neighbor.

live honorably by treating your body with respect.
live honorably by treating others with respect.

share God's boundless compassion with others.
be mindful of God's compassion in your life.

make a difference by your life.
influence others' lives by living well.

REFLECTION:

Which item do you need to work on to live well?
Whose example of living inspires you to live well?

"For the Lord takes pleasure in his people; he adorns the humble with salvation. Let the godly exult in glory; let them sing for joy on their beds."
~ Psalm 149:4-5 (ESV)

Christine M. Fisher

53

Painful Times

A friend texted me this picture and said, "Please excuse the awkward picture of my foot, but I just dropped my cell phone on it and look what happened. God's love during pain!"

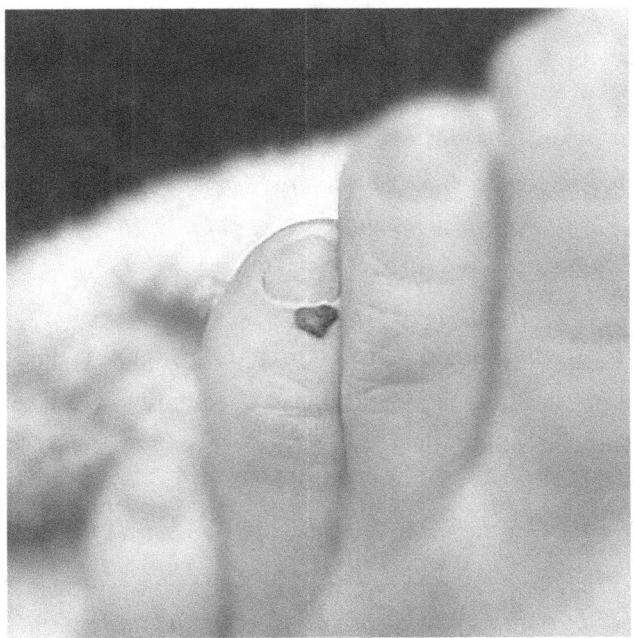

A perfectly shaped heart blood blister!

How could such a perfectly shaped heart blood blister appear on my friend's toe? The words "God's love during pain" echoed in my mind. What a perfect reminder that "God's love during pain" is with us.

This reminded me of Jesus. Consider the pain and suffering Jesus endured, particularly during His death. Jesus was obedient in fulfilling God's will.

Jesus had to endure pain and agony because of God's great love for us. We can spend eternity with Him because of the pain Jesus experienced.

> *"God showed how much he loved us by sending his one and only*
> *Son into the world so that we might have eternal life through*
> *him. This is real love—not that we loved God, but that he loved*
> *us and sent his Son as a sacrifice to take away our sins."*
> ~ 1 John 4:9-10 (NLT)

God loves you and me so much that He sent Jesus, His one and only Son, to earth as an atoning sacrifice for our sins. If we believe in Jesus as our Lord and Savior, we get to spend eternity in heaven. God's love at its finest.

> *"Christ suffered for our sins once for all time. He never sinned, but*
> *he died for sinners to bring you safely home to God. He suffered*
> *physical death, but he was raised to life in the Spirit."*
> ~ 1 Peter 3:18 (NLT)

Despite never having sinned, Christ suffered a brutal beating, hanging on a cross, and physical death. He did this in obedience to God, so we can go home to Him when He calls us.

> *"He is so rich in kindness and grace that he purchased our freedom with*
> *the blood of his Son* [Christ] *and forgave our sins. He has showered*
> *his kindness on us, along with all wisdom and understanding."*
> ~ Ephesians 1:7-8 (NLT)

It is the blood of Jesus that sets us free from our bonds of sin. God is full of kindness and grace, allowing us to have a way to choose salvation because of the blood Jesus shed for us.

When we suffer, whether physically, emotionally, or spiritually, may we remember that God's love is still with us. God never stopped loving Jesus, and God won't stop loving you or me. And, as my friend shared about the pain she experienced with her toe, it "is but a mere fraction of the pain my Savior endured for my sins."

Be encouraged during times of pain and suffering, knowing that...

> God's love is so great that He sent Jesus to set you free from your sins.
> Christ suffered a brutal death, so you can spend eternity with God.
> Christ's blood shed on the cross is a result of God's kindness and grace.
> it is a mere fraction of what Jesus endured for your sins.

REFLECTION:

What is the greatest pain or suffering you have endured?
Have you experienced God's love when in the throes of suffering?

> *"Dear friends, do not be surprised at the fiery ordeal that has come on you to test you, as though something strange were happening to you. But rejoice inasmuch as you participate in the sufferings of Christ, so that you may be overjoyed when his glory is revealed."*
> ~ 1 Peter 4:12-13

54

Life Lessons

It is fascinating to reflect on the fact that we are all made in God's image because of His infinite love and goodness for us human beings. Yet, God has given each of us special gifts, talents, and attributes so that no two of us are exactly alike. Our individual lives take different roads and are filled with different experiences, often dependent, to a great extent, on the families we are born into.

In God's mercy and compassion, He puts people and opportunities in our path to help us overcome obstacles that can change the trajectory of our lives. Sharing our stories brings encouragement and hope to others and is a way to form spiritual relationships. We learn from each other as we journey together.

At a retreat, a lady commented on a t-shirt I was wearing. That simple encounter led to a spiritual friendship. Now we take time to talk and meet for lunch despite living one and a half hours apart. Learning some of her story and seeing how she lives her faith encourages my faith journey and helps me see how I can grow more. She treats others with kindness and love, making them feel important and noticed, and offers strangers a friendly "Hello" or "God bless you."

At the restaurant where we meet, she knows several of the employees by name. I listened as she conversed with a young man. It sounded like he was a believer. I thought about offering him one of my 90-day devotionals, but I didn't follow through. When my friend and I met again, this same man took our order, and this time I followed through. He was in awe of meeting an author and said he wanted to show us something after his shift ended.

Christine M. Fisher

He pulled up a chair and, from his backpack, took out a book that he had recently self-published. Even more amazing was finding out that, while still in his twenties, he has published more than four books. It was a pleasure to listen to some of his story and to see the wisdom, well beyond his years, he has gained. His life has been quite challenging, yet he, like my lady friend, provides evidence that we can overcome obstacles or difficult circumstances in our lives. God's grace allows this to happen if we are open to it.

I reflected on three important takeaways from our conversations that day.

It is Important to Forgive People and Not Hold Grudges.

> *"Make allowance for each other's faults, and forgive anyone who offends you. Remember, the Lord forgave you, so you must forgive others."*
> ~ Colossians 3:13 (NLT)

It is important to forgive one another for the shortcomings we have. From the beginning, Adam and Eve sinned. God loves us all so much that He sent Jesus to earth as an atoning sacrifice, and His blood sets us free from our sins.

Sometimes we mess up big time. The hurts that are inflicted upon us may be unintentional, but they run deep, leaving us scarred. Can we let go of the deep hurts we have experienced and truly forgive others? Can we remember how Jesus endured such agony so we may live in freedom as we forgive others?

We Can Learn to Manage our Anger in Healthy Ways.

> *"And don't sin by letting anger control you. Don't let the sun go down while you are still angry, for anger gives a foothold to the devil."*
> ~ Ephesians 4:26-27 (NLT)

It is natural to feel anger. Paul, in his letter to the Ephesians, encourages us to make sure our anger does not control us and to release our anger daily. If we let anger build up, the evil one has a foothold to get us more and more off track and further from God.

As the restaurant employee shared, he learned to catch himself quicker when he gets angry, switching his mindset so that the anger does not control him. Saying a quick prayer asking God to help us release the anger, reminding ourselves that we all make mistakes, or calling on the name of Jesus will help us.

WE CAN OVERCOME OBSTACLES AND HARDSHIPS.

"Who shall separate us from the love of Christ? Shall trouble or hardship or persecution or famine or nakedness or danger or sword? As it is written: 'For your sake we face death all day long; we are considered as sheep to be slaughtered.' No, in all these things we are more than conquerors through him who loved us. For I am convinced that neither death nor life, neither angels nor demons, neither the present nor the future, nor any powers neither height nor depth, nor anything else in all creation, will be able to separate us from the love of God that is in Christ Jesus our Lord."
~ Romans 8:35-39

We can overcome obstacles and hardships because of God's great love for us. No matter what hardships we face, whether we lose all we have, like Job, or are persecuted, we are still victorious because we have Christ's love that is always present. His love cannot be taken from us; it is part of us.

The things of this earth, like what we eat, wear, or do, are only temporary. The one thing that lasts forever is the love of Christ and the victory we have with His love. Nothing in this world compares to Christ's love.

I remain in awe listening to people's stories and the deep heartache they have endured. My spirit is renewed when I hear how they have overcome adversity, in large part because of faith and God's grace. Often, a big factor is having someone believe in and offer them encouragement.

When one person speaks life into our spirit, it gives us courage and strength to know we can continue to grow. We can offer each other the gift of hope; we can make positive changes and be different as we spur one another on.

Be encouraged to…

> forgive others sincerely.
>> manage anger in healthy ways.
>>> work on overcoming obstacles and hardships with Christ's love.

> extend kindness and love to those you encounter.
>> take time to socialize and learn someone's story.
>>> reflect on lessons from someone you interact with.

REFLECTION:

Is there someone you can talk with to learn some of their story?
What lessons have you learned after hearing a friend's story?

> *"And Abraham's faith did not weaken, even though, at about 100 years of age, he figured his body was as good as dead—and so was Sarah's womb. Abraham never wavered in believing God's promise. In fact, his faith grew stronger, and in this he brought glory to God. He was fully convinced that God is able to do whatever he promises."*
> ~ Romans 4:19-21 (NLT)

55

Spiritual Gratitude

"Gratitude helps us see what is there instead of what isn't."
~ Annette Bridges

*"Focus more on being grateful for what you do have
rather than complaining about what you don't.
An attitude of gratitude will keep the blessings on the way."*
~ Mark Sutton

Do you, like me, find it easier to practice gratitude when everything is going well?
Isn't it harder to feel gratitude when we are going through rough waters and can't seem to catch a break?

How can we apply the wisdom of these quotes when we experience tougher times?

How can we be grateful for what we have?

What if your car breaks down and it takes a week for repairs?
Maybe you have the capacity to work at home.
Maybe you have a friend who goes in the same direction.

What if you have a health issue that requires surgery?
You appreciate the technological advances we have these days.
You recall the good health you've experienced.

What if you are struggling with forgiving yourself?

You may have friends who encourage you to "let go and let God."

You can talk with a religious official or therapist to work through forgiveness.

Paul is a good biblical example of living out gratitude despite difficult circumstances and never complaining. He originally persecuted Christians in the early church until Jesus appeared to him on the road to Damascus. Paul came to know that Jesus was the Lord, and his life took a complete turn. He became the most influential man who preached to the Gentiles, the non-Jewish people, and wrote many books in the New Testament.

In his ministry, Paul experienced being in prison, shipwrecked, and beaten. Do you know what helped him endure? His faith in Jesus was strong, and he had an attitude of gratitude, knowing what Jesus endured for him and for us. Paul prayed for his persecutors and shared the gospel with them because he wanted them to be saved.

"I am not saying this because I am in need, for I have learned to be content whatever the circumstances. I know what it is to be in need, and I know what it is to have plenty. I have learned the secret of being content in any and every situation, whether well fed or hungry, whether living in plenty or in want. I can do all this through him who gives me strength."
~ Philippians 4:11-13

No matter what Paul's physical surroundings or circumstances were, he lived with contentment. In his life, he experienced times of plenty and times of need. No matter what, he knew Jesus was in charge and would provide what he needed when he needed it. That kind of faith in Jesus' provision was only possible because Paul knew Jesus gave him strength to endure each moment.

What if we also look at gratitude on a spiritual level? What do we have that should fill us with gratitude?

GOD'S PRESENCE.

"This is my command—be strong and courageous! Do not be afraid or
discouraged. For the Lord your God is with you wherever you go."
~ Joshua 1:9 (NLT)

God's presence is always with us, every moment of every day. God is with
us in both the good and bad things that happen. Because He is always with
us, we can replace fear and discouragement with strength and courage.

GOD'S UNCONDITIONAL LOVE.

"God showed how much he loved us by sending his one and only
Son into the world so that we might have eternal life through
him. This is real love—not that we loved God, but that he loved
us and sent his Son as a sacrifice to take away our sins."
~ 1 John 4:9-10 (NLT)

God's pure love makes us His children. We cannot earn God's love; it is
just there. Our very being, our very existence, is because of God's love in
making us in His image. All we have to do is choose God and accept Jesus
as our Lord and Savior.

GOD'S PEACE.

"I am leaving you with a gift—peace of mind and heart. And the peace
I give is a gift the world cannot give. So don't be troubled or afraid."
~ John 14:27 (NLT)

In this troubled world, we can only have peace through Jesus. It is a peace
that sustains us despite troubling circumstances and even suffering. The
world does not provide peace.

May you be encouraged to look at events in life from more of a spiritual level than a worldly level. May we all have equal gratitude for our spirituality.

Be encouraged to…

focus on gratitude for the physical and spiritual things you have.
refrain from complaining about what is lacking.
keep gratitude at the forefront to continue the blessings that flow from above.
see God's presence surrounding you.
experience God's love through His messages to you.
let God's peace flow through your mind and heart.

REFLECTION:

Do you view the events in your life on a spiritual level?
What attribute of God above do you need to work on most?

> *"Oh give thanks to the Lord, for he is good; for his steadfast love endures forever! Say also: 'Save us, O God of our salvation, and gather and deliver us from among the nations, that we may give thanks to your holy name and glory in your praise.'"*
> ~ 1 Chronicles 16:34-35 (ESV)

56

Joyful Expectation

"I can't wait to open up a new page tomorrow
and see what God has in store for me."

This was the first thought, from a friend's text message, that popped into my head when I awoke the morning after having received God-filled, meaningful texts from him the day before.

He was referring to reading the next devotion in my book and seeing how God would make the message come alive. This man, a deacon, ministers to the residents of a nursing home daily, sharing Scripture along with a devotion from one of my books. He has shared with me how different devotions have related to a current event in his life. His sentence reminded me of this verse:

"The steadfast love of the Lord never ceases; his mercies never come to
an end; they are new every morning; great is your faithfulness."
~ Lamentations 3:22-23 (ESV)

God's love, mercy, and compassion for His people and promises never end. Each day, we are offered a fresh start to rejoice in seeing God and His faithfulness in our lives. He never gives up on us.

"I can't wait to open up a new page tomorrow
and see what God has in store for me."

When I first read that sentence, a parallel with our lives immediately came to mind. Yes, we should live each moment in joyful expectation of God

Christine M. Fisher

working in all of our circumstances, in both the good and the bad. I can't help but think that sentence is a great encouragement for us as we start afresh in God's presence each day.

We should greet each day with joyful expectation.
What does God have in store for my life today?
In what ways will He reveal Himself in my life?

Read these Scriptures about joyful expectation and ponder the question that follows:

"I wait for the Lord, my soul waits, and in his word, I hope;
my soul waits for the Lord more than watchmen for the
morning, more than watchmen for the morning."
~ Psalm 130:5-6 (ESV)

Be encouraged to wait for the Lord expectantly to work both in and through your life knowing you can trust His word and promises.

How can you share the joy of the Lord with a stranger?

"Don't burn out; keep yourselves fueled and aflame. Be alert servants
of the Master, cheerfully expectant. Don't quit in hard times; pray all
the harder. Help needy Christians; be inventive in hospitality."
~ Romans 12:11-13 (MSG)

As you go through daily events, pace yourself and keep the eyes of your heart open with joyful expectation to see how the Lord is working each circumstance out. He is present even in the most difficult of circumstances.

How can you let Him use you to impact another's life?

"Be still in the presence of the Lord, and wait patiently for him to act. Don't worry about evil people who prosper or fret about their wicked schemes."
~ Psalm 37:7 (NLT)

Be encouraged to take time to be still in the Lord's presence and wait to see Him act. The Lord is always with you, loving and protecting His precious child.

Who has God put in your path to help you follow Him more closely?

Greet each day with joyful expectation.

Be encouraged to...

> be mindful of how God is working in your circumstances.
> see each opportunity in life as a new start for God at work.
> share with others how God is orchestrating events in your life for His glory.

REFLECTION:

How has God provided during the darkest hours of the night?
What acts of service can you participate in to share God's love and presence?

> *"May you experience the love of Christ, though it is too great to understand fully. Then you will be made complete with all the fullness of life and power that comes from God. Now all glory to God, who is able, through his mighty power at work within us, to accomplish infinitely more than we might ask or think."*
> ~ Ephesians 3:19-20 (NLT)

Christine M. Fisher

57

Lasting Impressions

When I arrived at work, on my desk was a card and present from a coworker who was retiring. We had the opportunity to connect at work three months earlier, and I knew her as a kind, friendly, and helpful woman. One day I had an inkling to see if she would be interested in one of my books. Much to my surprise, she said she would like to see one. We had a lovely twenty minute conversation about faith and family, and she bought two of the books. About a month later, she bought the third book, and we shared more stories about our lives. What a blessing to encourage one another with understanding and empathy.

It was ironic to realize that, in 2016, I had taken a picture of two items on her desk without her knowing. These items fit with a reflection I was writing for my website. (I am always on the lookout for inspiring pictures that might one day be in one of my reflections.) What a blessing, seven years later, to receive the one below from her as a memento of our friendship.

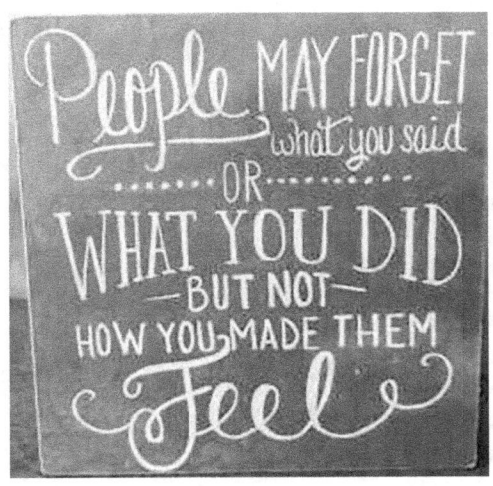

Isn't it important to remember the impact our lives have on others? Isn't it most important to realize how we make people **feel** that is of paramount importance?

I couldn't help but think of Jesus and how He made people feel. Consider this Bible story:

> *"But Jesus went to the Mount of Olives. At dawn he appeared again in the temple courts, where all the people gathered around him, and he sat down to teach them. The teachers of the law and the Pharisees brought in a woman caught in adultery. They made her stand before the group and said to Jesus, 'Teacher, this woman was caught in the act of adultery. In the Law Moses commanded us to stone such women. Now what do you say?' They were using this question as a trap, in order to have a basis for accusing him. But Jesus bent down and started to write on the ground with his finger. When they kept on questioning him, he straightened up and said to them, 'Let any one of you who is without sin be the first to throw a stone at her.' Again he stooped down and wrote on the ground. At this, those who heard began to go away one at a time, the older ones first, until only Jesus was left, with the woman still standing there. Jesus straightened up and asked her, 'Woman, where are they? Has no one condemned you?' 'No one, sir,' she said. 'Then neither do I condemn you,' Jesus declared. 'Go now and leave your life of sin.'"*
> ~ John 8:1-11

Did Jesus make the adulterous woman feel ashamed?

   Did Jesus show hatred toward her even though she was caught in sin?

         Did Jesus use cutting remarks to dehumanize others?

The answer to all these questions is no. Rather, Jesus made her feel valued, loved, and respected as He told her to leave her current life of sin. Jesus treated the teachers of the law and the Pharisees with value, love, and respect in the same way by gently helping them see that they, too, were sinners.

Do we Make People Feel Valued?

"Then God said, 'Let us make mankind in our image, in our likeness, so that they may rule over the fish in the sea and the birds in the sky, over the livestock and all the wild animals, and over all the creatures that move along the ground.' So God created mankind in his own image, in the image of God he created them; male and female he created them."
~ Genesis 1:26-27

What a privilege to be made in God's very image! It is important to remind ourselves of that fact each day. Do we take time to consider that what we think of as the worst person is also made in God's image? God is perfect, and in His eyes, we are all of equal value. God does not have any favorites.

In what specific way can you make one person feel valued?

Do We Make People Feel Loved for Who They Are?

"A new command I give you: Love one another. As I have loved you, so you must love one another. By this everyone will know that you are my disciples, if you love one another."
~ John 13:34-35

As disciples of Jesus, we are given the command to love one another purely because they, too, are children of God. God never stops loving us, even when we are steeped in sin. We need to model that same love for others, even when we think they don't deserve it. It is possible that our modeling of love can lead another to the first step in their conversion.

Is there someone you can be challenged to love unconditionally, realizing they, too, are a child of God?

DO WE INCLUDE ALL PEOPLE, MAKING THEM FEEL RESPECTED?

"If one part suffers, every part suffers with it; if one part
is honored, every part rejoices with it. Now you are the
body of Christ, and each one of you is a part of it."
~ 1 Corinthians 12:26-27

We, the body of Christ, are all individual members with different gifts and talents that God has given us. Each of our gifts is equally important and necessary for the body of Christ to function properly. When one of us experiences suffering or joy, we all join in. One of our responsibilities is to make every part of the body feel respected and included.

Can you try to speak to someone outside your normal circle of friends?

Be encouraged to...

> see the value in every face you encounter, knowing they are a child of God.
> model the unconditional love God has for you.
> respect people, especially those who might have different views than you.

REFLECTION:

What did someone do that made you feel valued and respected?
Whose eyes can you look into and tell them you see Jesus in them?

"In him we have obtained an inheritance, having been
predestined according to the purpose of him who works all things
according to the counsel of his will, so that we who were the
first to hope in Christ might be to the praise of his glory."
~ Ephesians 1:11-12 (ESV)

Christine M. Fisher

58

Right Timing

A friend shared that she was wondering about God's purpose for her life. I pointed out that our purpose is even found in the little things, in the way we show kindness and love to others. Our purpose does not have to be grand in the world's eyes. God knows our hearts, and the condition of our hearts is what is most important. God can use us all if we allow Him to.

Wherever you are right now,
whatever you are doing,
the present is the time,
where God can use you,
to be of service to Him.

"There was a small town with only a few people, and a great king came with his army and besieged it. A poor, wise man knew how to save the town, and so it was rescued. But afterward no one thought to thank him. So even though wisdom is better than strength, those who are wise will be despised if they are poor. What they say will not be appreciated for long. Better to hear the quiet words of a wise person than the shouts of a foolish king."
~ Ecclesiastes 9:14-17 (NLT)

In this Scripture, we learn that a poor man, filled with wisdom, saved a town despite a king who had a great army. We learn that wisdom is more important than strength. God can use anyone who is willing, even the lowly. People might think that riches and power are most valuable, but it is the humble servant who is important in God's eyes.

Last year, I decided to pay my taxes in person. As I was coming out of the building, I saw a lady I had known many years ago. We embraced as soon as we saw each other and then we spent a few minutes catching up on our lives. I mentioned the books I recently published, thinking she already knew about them. She was delighted to pick one from the supply in my car, and we embraced again before departing. I marveled at how God orchestrated the meeting through my simple act of deciding to pay the taxes in person.

> *"The people you rescued by your great power and strong hand are your servants. O Lord, please hear my prayer! Listen to the prayers of those of us who delight in honoring you. Please grant me success today by making the king favorable to me. Put it into his heart to be kind to me. In those days I was the king's cupbearer."*
> ~ Nehemiah 1:10-11 (NLT)

> *"The king asked, 'Well, how can I help you?' With a prayer to the God of heaven, I replied, 'If it please the king, and if you are pleased with me, your servant, send me to Judah to rebuild the city where my ancestors are buried.'"*
> ~ Nehemiah 2:4-5 (NLT)

We see that Nehemiah, a Jewish high official in the Persian court, was faith-filled in praying for the people of Jerusalem. We see in his heart that he cared about others. Nehemiah was King Artaxerxes' personal cupbearer, which meant he checked all the king's food and drink before the king was allowed to ingest it to make sure it had not been poisoned. This shows us that Nehemiah was trustworthy and in a respected position.

The land of Judah lay in ruins after being destroyed by fire, which saddened Nehemiah, who had a compassionate heart. King Artaxerxes granted him permission to go to Jerusalem where he helped organize and rebuild the city walls of Jerusalem after the Babylonian exile. God allowed Nehemiah, a more prominent person, to be in the right place at the right time to help the Jewish people.

As a retirement present for my dental hygienist a few years ago, I gave her one of my books. We keep in touch every now and then via text. One day I asked her if she thought the dentist would appreciate a book and she said she wasn't sure. Later, I ran into the hygienist at a store, and she said, "Yes, the dentist is interested in a book." The next week, I left a book for him at the office. It was a lovely blessing to get a note from him saying God is using the book to give him some guidance and renew his faith, which has been lacking.

God made you who you are
> and placed you where you are
>> because where you are
>>> needs who you are.

Be encouraged, knowing…

God will use you right where you are.
> you are always in service to God.
>> God uses everyone who is willing.

wisdom is better than strength.
> your heart is what counts.
>> God's timing is always perfect.

Can you look at events in your life, even the simple ones, and know you were in the right place at the right time? I see those times as God's orchestrations. Sometimes we can easily see the bigger orchestrations, but just as important are the smaller ones because we never know how God will use them in someone else's life.

REFLECTION:

When did you know God had you in the right place at the right time?
Is your heart open and willing to let God use you in any capacity He
chooses?

> *"Declare his glory among the nations, his marvelous works*
> *among all the peoples! For great is the Lord, and greatly*
> *to be praised; he is to be feared above all gods."*
> ~ Psalm 96:3-4 (ESV)

59

Growing in Love

"Instead, we will speak the truth in love, growing in every way more and more like Christ, who is the head of his body, the church. He makes the whole body fit together perfectly. As each part does its own special work, it helps the other parts grow, so that the whole body is healthy and growing and full of love."
~ Ephesians 4:15-16 (NLT)

We all belong to Christ, who is the head of the body of believers. That makes us members of the body of Christ. What a privilege that is. God has given each of us special gifts to share with the body of Christ to help build it into a stronger unit. With each of us doing our part, we help each member grow in love and become stronger in faith.

Do you often think you have nothing to offer others?
Do you wonder how you can make a difference?
Do you feel like you aren't growing?

Know that with every prayer you offer, every act of kindness, and every time you reach out to encourage someone, you make a difference in the body of Christ. Whether you are young or old, rich or poor, you can help the body of Christ grow in love and be healthier. The little things done in love have a great impact.

I was reflecting on a dear friend who has endured much suffering and continual pain for more than half of his 82 years on this earth. He has been wheelchair-bound for many years now, and his beautiful wife continues to take loving care of him.

Recently, he fell and was admitted to the hospital. Upon admission, he tested positive for COVID, though he was asymptomatic. They placed him in the ICU where he was quarantined for ten days. They were ten long, lonely, dark days with no trace of outside light or physical contact with people. My heart ached for him and what he was enduring.

I have always been amazed at his positive attitude throughout the years, despite his circumstances. He is the perfect example of doing his part to help members of the body of Christ grow in love. Through the years, he has tutored many students, helping them succeed and believe in themselves. He has been known to call widows weekly to check on them. In fact, despite being in isolation, he kept to his schedule and reached out to at least one of them, just like clockwork. He sends encouraging notes to let people know he is praying for them, and he has helped many students increase their knowledge by providing scholarships.

How have you helped someone during a dark time in their journey?

In the last three years or so, my life has been growing in love and with a deeper relationship with the Spirit because of the people God is putting in my path. Conversing with people strengthens my faith, challenges me to go deeper, and helps me see ways I can grow. God is filling me with more love for myself and for the body of Christ. By sharing our stories and hearts, we can encourage and learn from one another. As a friend says, "We never travel alone."

We all go through rough patches where we need a little more intervention from our fellow pilgrims. It is important to reach out in honesty to let a trusted person know when we are struggling with life. That is what the body of Christ is for. We can speak truth and life to encourage someone when they cannot make it on their own.

Christine M. Fisher

Have you taken time to thank someone you can trust and share with when you are at your lowest point?

Be encouraged to…

grow more like Christ in sharing love.
remember that you are a special member of the body of Christ that fits perfectly.
do your special part so the body grows in love and is healthier.

challenge yourself to reach out in love to someone.
reflect on how you are growing in love.
see how you can contribute to the health of the body of Christ.

REFLECTION:

What is one of your gifts to the body of Christ?
Who and what gift have you been a recipient of?

"Or do you not know that your body is a temple of the Holy Spirit within you, whom you have from God? You are not your own, for you were bought with a price. So glorify God in your body."
~ 1 Corinthians 6:19-20 (ESV)

60

Stranger Blessings

I was at a church event where the leader mentioned there was a gentleman at his table who would be returning to Florida, where he lives. During the prayer time, the man from Florida shared a prayer request, which gave me an inkling to share one of my books with him. At the end of the event, he was talking with a couple of people, and I didn't want to interrupt him, so I was about to leave. But then, a lady next to me asked, "Did you bring your book to give to someone specific or just in case you needed one?" I replied, "Well, thanks for asking; it was just in case. At prayer time, I felt I was supposed to give it to the man from Florida. Thanks for inspiring me to follow up on that inkling."

After approaching him, we talked for forty minutes before departing. It felt like the Holy Spirit was welling up in me as I shared more and more about my faith and writing journey. He understood completely and shared some of his story. I showed him the prayer garden, where I spent many days reflecting on God. It was near my car, where I was inspired to share another book with him. Before we left the prayer garden, he prayed for us both, and we shared our contact information so we could stay in touch.

> *"We loved you so much that we shared with you not*
> *only God's Good News but our own lives, too."*
> ~ 1 Thessalonians 2:8 (NLT)

What a delight and joy to share God's good news and His work in our lives. Two strangers, united in Christ, experienced an instant spiritual connection.

Christine M. Fisher

Two days after that first encounter, he shared via text, "I realized something Thursday night in our conversation—I wanted to hear more. Here's what I learned. I pray daily for God to bring people into my life—to see with my spiritual eyes and hear with my spiritual ears the needs of others—to minister to their needs and help them along this journey. But I'm not sure I've prayed for Jesus to bring someone into my life specifically to minister to me. It's not a pride thing, I don't believe, but rather just not an awareness. Then you came along. You took a chance to meet a stranger—to open up and share. Thank you, Christine. You are wonderfully made. Anyway, for sure, God has brought people into my life to journey with and help me and I am always thankful. But you brought that awareness to me that I should pray for Him to bring people to minister to me."

Let's take a few minutes to reflect on a few of the thoughts this man shared:

ARE YOU OPEN TO TALKING WITH A STRANGER ABOUT GOD WHEN YOU GET A PROMPTING?

> *"Do not forget to show hospitality to strangers, for by so doing some*
> *people have shown hospitality to angels without knowing it."*
> ~ Hebrews 13:2

We don't know what people are going through. We may never know the impact of a seemingly simple gesture on someone's life until we get to heaven. You may even find out that your simple "Hello" at 6 p.m. one day was the first time the person was spoken to that day. Sharing our God-encounters with a stranger can breathe life into both our spirits.

DON'T WE OFTEN MINISTER TO OR TRY TO HELP MEET OTHERS' NEEDS AS WE PLACE OTHERS BEFORE OURSELVES?

> *"Do not neglect to do good and to share what you*
> *have, for such sacrifices are pleasing to God."*
> ~ Hebrews 13:16 (ESV)

Indeed, God wants us to do good to others, especially those in need. We can share our time, talents, and treasures to help others. When we share from the goodness of our hearts, knowing we are following God's will, God is well pleased with us. Our sacrifices are a way we can give back to God.

Do We Pray for People to Come into Our Lives to Minister to us Spiritually?

> *"As iron sharpens iron, so one person sharpens another."*
> ~ Proverbs 27:17

Do we tend to focus on our personal needs for spirituality? God desires that we build loving and growing relationships with like-minded people to help us grow even more spiritually. When we are like iron for each other, we can be used to help each other grow in faith and character and have honest conversations about ways we can improve. We can become more and more like God as we are continually changing.

Be encouraged to…

> follow the prompting to entertain a stranger in whatever capacity.
> seek ways to minister or help meet others' needs.
> pray for and be aware of spiritual ministers who come into your life.
> see how you can be like iron challenging others to grow spiritually.

My prayer for you is what this man shared in a later text: "Jesus, help me especially to be so aware when you bring someone into my life to minister to me."

REFLECTION:

What random encounter with a stranger became a spiritual friend?
Have you prayed for God to send someone to minister to you?

> *"Therefore welcome one another as Christ has*
> *welcomed you, for the glory of God."*
> ~ Romans 15:7 (ESV)

Section 3

GOD'S GLORY MANIFESTED IN JESUS

"For God, who said, 'Let there be light in the darkness,' has made this light shine in our hearts so we could know the glory of God that is seen in the face of Jesus Christ."
~ 2 Corinthians 4:6 (NLT)

To have a plan for our redemption once Adam and Eve sinned, God sent His only Son, Jesus, to earth as an atoning sacrifice for all who would believe in Him. Jesus, being God's Son, is both human and divine. Jesus walked this earth and experienced many of the same human interactions we do. He can relate to what we go through.

Jesus couldn't help but manifest God's glory while He lived on earth. During His three years of public ministry, He healed many and shared unconditional love, compassion, and mercy. Jesus suffered a brutal death, being beaten and nailed to a cross. His face was beaten and bloody, yet God's glory was still manifested. The great love of Jesus for being obedient to His Father for our sake shone forth. Nothing could stop the light from shining.

God's glory manifested in Jesus.

"The glory of God is revealed in the face of Jesus."
~ Fr. Mike Schmitz

61

Glorified Body

We know that three days after Jesus' death, He rose from the dead on that first Easter morning. During the next forty days, the risen Jesus appeared to different people before He ascended into heaven. Jesus, in His glorified, resurrected body, appeared to Mary Magdalene, eleven of His disciples, the two disciples on the road to Emmaus, and Thomas, among others.

What do we learn about Jesus' glorified body?

JESUS HAD FLESH AND BONES.

> *"While they were still talking about this, Jesus himself stood among them and said to them, 'Peace be with you.' They were startled and frightened, thinking they saw a ghost. He said to them, 'Why are you troubled, and why do doubts rise in your minds? Look at my hands and my feet. It is I myself! Touch me and see; a ghost does not have flesh and bones, as you see I have.'"*
> ~ Luke 24:36-39

JESUS COULD STILL EAT.

> *"When he had said this, he showed them his hands and feet. And while they still did not believe it because of joy and amazement, he asked them, 'Do you have anything here to eat?' They gave him a piece of broiled fish, and he took it and ate it in their presence."*
> ~ Luke 24:40-43

JESUS STILL HAD SCARS FROM THE NAILS WHEN HE WAS CRUCIFIED.

"A week later his disciples were in the house again, and Thomas was with them. Though the doors were locked, Jesus came and stood among them and said, 'Peace be with you!' Then he said to Thomas, 'Put your finger here; see my hands. Reach out your hand and put it into my side. Stop doubting and believe.' Thomas said to him, 'My Lord and my God!'"
~ John 20:26-28

JESUS COULD APPEAR AND VANISH WHENEVER HE WANTED.

"When he was at the table with them [the two disciples on the road to Emmaus], *he took bread, gave thanks, broke it and began to give it to them. Then their eyes were opened and they recognized him, and he disappeared from their sight. They asked each other, 'Were not our hearts burning within us while he talked with us on the road and opened the Scriptures to us?'"*
~ Luke 24:30-32

Isn't God amazing with how He made all of creation and our bodies? He breathed life into Adam and continues to breathe life into us. He sent Jesus, His only Son, who was both divine and human, to earth to experience all we do, except Jesus was sinless. Jesus died, rose three days later, and appeared with a glorified body. We, too, will one day experience a glorified body, just like Jesus.

"But our citizenship is in heaven, and from it we await a Savior, the Lord Jesus Christ, who will transform our lowly body to be like his glorious body, by the power that enables him even to subject all things to himself."
~ Philippians 3:20-21 (ESV)

What do we learn about Jesus' messages when He appears in His glorified body?

JESUS IS ALWAYS CALLING OUR NAME, EVEN IN OUR SADNESS AND
BROKENNESS.

*"Now Mary stood outside the tomb crying. As she wept, she bent over to look
into the tomb and saw two angels in white, seated where Jesus' body had
been, one at the head and the other at the foot. They asked her, 'Woman,
why are you crying?' 'They have taken my Lord away,' she said, 'and I
don't know where they have put him.' At this, she turned around and saw
Jesus standing there, but she did not realize that it was Jesus. He asked her,
'Woman, why are you crying? Who is it you are looking for?' Thinking he
was the gardener, she said, 'Sir, if you have carried him away, tell me where
you have put him, and I will get him.' Jesus said to her, 'Mary.' She turned
toward him and cried out in Aramaic, 'Rabboni!' (which means 'Teacher')."*
~ John 20:11-16

Mary was very distraught when she saw the empty tomb. She wanted to
find out who stole Jesus' body. She loved Jesus for the way He changed
her life by driving out seven demons. Mary did not physically recognize
Jesus because He was in His glorified state, but as soon as He called her
name, she knew Jesus was standing in front of her. Jesus came to bring her
comfort when her heart was broken.

JESUS SAYS, "PEACE BE WITH YOU," EVEN WHEN FEAR STARTS TO OVERTAKE US.

*"On the evening of that first day of the week, when the disciples were
together, with the doors locked for fear of the Jewish leaders, Jesus came
and stood among them and said, 'Peace be with you!' After he said this,
he showed them his hands and side. The disciples were overjoyed when
they saw the Lord. Again Jesus said, 'Peace be with you! As the Father
has sent me, I am sending you.' And with that he breathed on them
and said, 'Receive the Holy Spirit. If you forgive anyone's sins, their
sins are forgiven; if you do not forgive them, they are not forgiven.'"*
~ John 20:19-23

The disciples were hiding behind the locked doors because they feared for their lives after Jesus was put to death. They were afraid it might happen to them too. How beautiful that Jesus' first message is *"Peace be with you!"* Jesus' peace brings us joy, just as the disciples experienced it. Jesus then commissioned the disciples by breathing the Holy Spirit into them.

JESUS' GLORIFIED BODY CARRIES THE WOUNDS HE ENDURED, SO WE CAN STOP DOUBTING AND BELIEVE HE IS THE SAVIOR OF THE WORLD.

> *"A week later his disciples were in the house again, and Thomas was with them. Though the doors were locked, Jesus came and stood among them and said, 'Peace be with you!' Then he said to Thomas, 'Put your finger here; see my hands. Reach out your hand and put it into my side. Stop doubting and believe.' Thomas said to him, 'My Lord and my God!' Then Jesus told him, 'Because you have seen me, you have believed; blessed are those who have not seen and yet have believed.' Jesus performed many other signs in the presence of his disciples, which are not recorded in this book. But these are written that you may believe that Jesus is the Messiah, the Son of God, and that by believing you may have life in his name."*
> ~ John 20:26-31

Thomas was not with the other disciples when the risen Jesus first appeared to them. He could not believe that the others had seen Jesus, as no one had ever risen from the dead before. Jesus cared for Thomas and wanted him to experience seeing Him firsthand. He knew that by making Thomas touch His wounds, he would never doubt again. How blessed are we who have not had the privilege of physically touching Jesus' wounds but believe.

JESUS IS PRESENT TO US IN THE SCRIPTURES AND IN THE BREAKING OF BREAD, EVEN WHEN WE ARE DOWNCAST AND FEEL ALONE.

> *"He said to them, 'How foolish you are, and how slow to believe all that the prophets have spoken! Did not the Messiah have to suffer*

these things and then enter his glory?' And beginning with Moses and all the Prophets, he explained to them what was said in all the Scriptures concerning himself. As they approached the village to which they were going, Jesus continued on as if he were going farther. But they urged him strongly, 'Stay with us, for it is nearly evening; the day is almost over.' So he went in to stay with them. When he was at the table with them, he took bread, gave thanks, broke it and began to give it to them. Then their eyes were opened and they recognized him, and he disappeared from their sight. They asked each other, 'Were not our hearts burning within us while he talked with us on the road and opened the Scriptures to us?'"

~ Luke 24:25-32

The two disciples on the road to Emmaus were trying to flee from Jerusalem for fear of being persecuted. They were downcast because they thought Jesus, the One who was going to redeem Israel, was dead. The disciples did not recognize Jesus as the One they were conversing with because of His glorified state. Once Jesus started explaining the Scriptures to them, they realized who He was. Jesus' identity was also revealed to them through the breaking of the bread. There was no doubt Jesus was alive.

Be encouraged to…

> take time to marvel at the miracle of Jesus' glorified body.
> > hear Jesus call your name when you feel broken.
> > > hear Jesus say "Peace to you" when fear starts to overtake you.

> touch Jesus' wounds that He suffered for you.
> > listen to Jesus in the Scriptures.
> > > experience Jesus in the breaking of the bread.

REFLECTION:

Does knowing you will have a glorified body like Jesus fill you with awe? What message from Jesus' glorified body resonates most with you?

"We were therefore buried with him through baptism into death in order that, just as Christ was raised from the dead through the glory of the Father, we too may live a new life. For if we have been united with him in a death like his, we will certainly also be united with him in a resurrection like his."
~ Romans 6:4-5

Christine M. Fisher

62

Worship

I had just arrived at my prayer garden one day when my phone rang. It was my son using his buddy's phone. This son is quite skilled at prefacing things appropriately to make sure I knew the most important details first. The first words I heard were, "I am okay. Everyone is okay. Everything is okay."

He had been longboarding with a friend and fell off, which resulted in the left side of his body being scraped up. They had assessed the situation with another friend, and he was seeking medical treatment when he finally contacted me. He needed three stitches in his chin, but the fat lip, blue eye, scrapped-up shoulder and hip on his left side made him look like he had been in quite the battle.

The thoughts from a sermon came to his mind as soon as the accident happened.

Our worship should not be a distraction from our circumstances.
Worship, no matter the circumstances.

As my son and his friend were driving to get assessed, they turned on Christian worship music and he kept worshiping the Lord despite the circumstances.

When the physician assistant went to stitch up his chin, my son focused on praying and said he did not feel anything. When he returned home, he was giving praise to the Lord for sparing him from a much worse outcome, knowing he was fortunate to only need three stitches, with no broken bones. God has more work for him to do here on this earth, he concluded.

I was reminded of a good way to worship and pray using the letters in the word ACTS.

> **A**doration–Let the Lord know the deep love and respect you have for Him. Praise God.
> **C**onfession–Admit that you are a sinner and that you need God's forgiveness.
> **T**hanksgiving–Thank the Lord for His goodness in your life.
> **S**upplication–Bring your needs to the Lord, the prayers that are weighing heavy on your heart.

Keep in mind...

> our worship should not be a distraction from our circumstances.
> to worship, no matter the circumstances.
> to worship continually in all things.

REFLECTION:

When was the last time you worshipped despite difficult circumstances? Which of the four types of prayer do you tend to neglect?

> *"Ascribe to the Lord the glory due his name; worship the Lord in the splendor of his holiness."*
> ~ Psalm 29:2

63

Servanthood

I was at the closing celebration of a weekend event where I felt led to serve others in the setup, cleanup, and serving of meals in the dining room. This was the first time I had helped at this location, and the words I thought of as I served were,

> Serve as if it is the first time you served; serve
> as if it is your **only** time serving.

I thought about how Jesus was the ultimate servant, who came to earth to serve, not to be served. I envisioned Jesus doing even the most menial of tasks, like wiping food off of chairs, vacuuming the crumbs off the floor, and emptying the garbage, with love and humility. Jesus thought no task was without value, especially when done in love and humility. Jesus did not think He was above anyone or that He was exempt from doing menial tasks.

Whenever I serve, I try to be attentive and offer assistance to what others may need in the task they are performing. It can be as simple as giving them a utensil when their hands are full or consolidating food into one container so the dishwasher can scrub the baked-on lasagna pan.

I was grateful to be able to serve others that weekend, especially since I was one of the younger people. Though I didn't know any of the people there, I felt welcome, sharing hugs with the main lady, who was happy I came to help. It is a blessing to talk with other people, to try to see why they have the perspectives they have due to their life experiences, and to share Christ with them.

One lady took me under her wing and filled me in on how things worked, where things were, and the history of things. She blessed me in our interactions, and her willingness to extend herself by sharing with me helped me realize the importance of reaching out to newcomers when I'm working at my local soup kitchen.

Servanthood is a way of life. Looking for even the littlest ways to serve others is something Jesus did while on this earth. No matter what we do, we need to do it in love and because of Christ in us. May we strive to be more like Jesus every day by serving others with love and humility.

REFLECTION:

Do you feel God nudging you to serve others in a new capacity? What way have you served others that has blessed you most?

"I have brought you glory on earth by finishing the work you gave me to do." ~ John 17:4

64

Sacrifice

Does it seem like your faith, trust, and love of God are tested almost daily? How well do you fare in obedience to the Lord? God provides a great example for us in the man Abraham.

"Some time later, God tested Abraham's faith. 'Abraham!' God called. 'Yes,' he replied. 'Here I am.' 'Take your son, your only son—yes, Isaac, whom you love so much—and go to the land of Moriah. Go and sacrifice him as a burnt offering on one of the mountains, which I will show you.'"
~ Genesis 22:1-2 (NLT)

Abraham and Sarah were barren and childless until they were in their 90s, way past their childbearing years, when God blessed them with the gift of Isaac. After waiting so long for a child, imagine hearing God say to offer that child as a burnt offering to the Lord. Would you be obedient?

God tests our faith just as He tested Abraham's faith. Notice that God tests our faith, whereas Satan tries to tempt us, hoping to make us fall. God is interested in knowing our sincerity of faith and commitment to Him.

When Abraham responded to God's voice with "Here I am," he was responding as a servant does. He knows God is God, and he is His humble servant.

Think how Jesus, in His humanity, was tested to see if He would follow through in obedience to go to the cross for your sins and mine. Jesus was the perfect example throughout His whole life of being a servant, even to the point of death. God sacrificed Jesus, His one and only Son, for us so we could spend eternity in heaven. It is interesting to learn that the land of Moriah, where Abraham was ready to sacrifice Isaac, is very close to the place where Jesus was crucified.

> *"The next morning Abraham got up early. He saddled his donkey and took two of his servants with him, along with his son, Isaac. Then he chopped wood for a fire for a burnt offering and set out for the place God had told him about. On the third day of their journey, Abraham looked up and saw the place in the distance."*
> ~ Genesis 22:3-4 (NLT)

Abraham took two of his servants, along with Isaac, to the place God told him. The journey took three days of travel. The burnt offering, the sacrifice Abraham was to provide to God, required wood from trees.

Jesus, being the ultimate sacrifice, carried the wood of the cross on His way to Calvary. When Jesus hung on the cross, there were two thieves crucified, one on each side. After dying, Jesus rose on the third day. What striking similarities there are to Abraham's story.

> *"So Abraham placed the wood for the burnt offering on Isaac's shoulders, while he himself carried the fire and the knife…"*
> ~ Genesis 22:6 (NLT)

On the way to the mountain where Abraham was to sacrifice Isaac, Isaac carried the wood on his shoulders.

As Jesus walked the road that led to His crucifixion, He carried a heavy wooden cross on His shoulders.

> *"Isaac spoke up and said to his father Abraham, 'Father?' 'Yes, my son?' Abraham replied. 'The fire and wood are here,' Isaac said, 'but where is the lamb for the burnt offering?' Abraham*

answered, 'God himself will provide the lamb for the burnt
offering, my son.' And the two of them went on together."
~ Genesis 22:7-8

Through all of this, Isaac did not realize he was the burnt offering God was asking Abraham to sacrifice. What faith Abraham continued to exhibit, knowing God would provide the perfect burnt offering.

God did indeed provide the perfect lamb for the ultimate sacrifice. God provided His only Son, Jesus, who is the perfect Lamb of God.

"When they arrived at the place where God had told him to go, Abraham
built an altar and arranged the wood on it. Then he tied his son, Isaac,
and laid him on the altar on top of the wood. And Abraham picked up
the knife to kill his son as a sacrifice. At that moment the angel of the
Lord called to him from heaven, 'Abraham! Abraham!' 'Yes,' Abraham
replied. 'Here I am!' 'Don't lay a hand on the boy!' the angel said. 'Do
not hurt him in any way, for now I know that you truly fear God.
You have not withheld from me even your son, your only son.'"
~ Genesis 22: 9-12 (NLT)

"Abraham never wavered in believing God's promise. In fact, his
faith grew stronger, and in this he brought glory to God."
~ Romans 4:20 (NLT)

Abraham, in faith and obedience, did what God instructed. Abraham was faithful and willing to obey God, no matter the request. God saw his sincerity of heart and did not allow him to sacrifice Isaac. Since Abraham's faith did not waver, it grew even stronger, and more glory was given to God.

Jesus was faithful and, in obedience to God, sacrificed His life for our sins. Jesus, despite the agony He endured in dying, was sincere in being the sacrificial offering for all mankind. Jesus' life and sacrifice give all glory and honor to God.

Be encouraged to reflect on the story of Abraham and Jesus, seeing the ways they exemplified obedience to God. Take time to reflect on your life to see the ways you can improve in faith, trust, love, and obedience to God. It is important to know that obedience might come before understanding. We do not always understand why God wants us to do some things, but we need to be obedient.

May God help increase your faith, trust, and love in Him.

May God help you see the times when He wants you to be obedient to Him.

REFLECTION:

Is there something the Lord is calling you to be obedient to that you have been avoiding?
How have you been blessed to walk in obedience in a situation?

"And being found in appearance as a man, he humbled himself by becoming obedient to death—even death on a cross! Therefore, God exalted him to the highest place and gave him the name that is above every name, that at the name of Jesus every knee should bow, in heaven and on earth and under the earth, and every tongue acknowledge that Jesus Christ is Lord, to the glory of God the Father. Therefore, my dear friends, as you have always obeyed—not only in my presence, but now much more in my absence—continue to work out your salvation with fear and trembling..."
~ Philippians 2:8-12

65

There is Hope

Shattered dreams,
>   broken hearts,
>>   lonely people pass us by every day.

People without hope,
>   searching for happiness,
>>   a lost and dying world.

What can we offer these people?

The world offers happiness to them in the form of riches, fame, sex, drugs, and alcohol. But the world's happiness does not bring anything to place our hope in, for these worldly pleasures last but a few fleeting moments. They don't offer anything lasting and real, and there is nothing to cling to.

Our only true hope is found in and through Jesus Christ. With Christ as the center of our lives, we can possess a lasting happiness that will carry us through life. Christ gives us a peace that surpasses all understanding, despite the trials we may be facing. He is our best friend and will never leave us, even though others may desert us.

Our greatest hope is in the day we will meet Jesus face-to-face and spend eternity with Him. Christ is the lasting hope we can offer people as we live and walk it each day.

"If only for this life we have hope in Christ, we
are of all people most to be pitied."
~ 1 Corinthians 15:19

Christ is the hope we need to offer others; it will change their lives forever. The song *Cry Out to Jesus* by Third Day, talks about the hope Jesus provides. Let these words penetrate your heart and soul.

There is **hope** for the helpless.
Rest for the weary.
And **love** for the brokenhearted.[2]

REFLECTION:

Who can you share Jesus' message of hope with?
How did Jesus provide hope in a situation in your life?

"To them God has chosen to make known among the Gentiles the glorious
riches of this mystery, which is Christ in you, the hope of glory."
~ Colossians 1:27

66

Marvel

"But Peter rose and ran to the tomb; stooping and looking
in, he saw the linen cloths by themselves; and he went
*home **marveling** at what had happened."*
~ Luke 24:12 (ESV)

We are given the detail that, after seeing with his own eyes that Jesus' tomb was empty, Peter *"marveled."* Jesus had risen from the dead, and Peter, along with the other disciples, would see Jesus in His glorified state at different times over the course of the next forty days.

A Google definition of marvel is: "to be filled with wonder or astonishment."
A biblical definition of marvel is: "a person's reaction to a supernatural act of God."

What other Scriptures share stories about people who marveled at different things?

JESUS' PARENTS, MARY AND JOSEPH, MARVELED!

"Now there was a man in Jerusalem, whose name was Simeon,
and this man was righteous and devout, waiting for the
consolation of Israel, and the Holy Spirit was upon him. And it
had been revealed to him by the Holy Spirit that he would not
see death before he had seen the Lord's Christ. And he came in
the Spirit into the temple, and when the parents brought in the
child Jesus, to do for him according to the custom of the Law,
he took him up in his arms and blessed God and said, 'Lord,

> *now you are letting your servant depart in peace, according to*
> *your word; for my eyes have seen your salvation that you have*
> *prepared in the presence of all peoples, a light for revelation to*
> *the Gentiles, and for glory to your people Israel.' And his father*
> *and his mother **marveled** at what was said about him."*
> ~ Luke 2:25-33 (ESV)

The Holy Spirit revealed to Simeon that before he died, he would see the Salvation of the world. When Mary's time of purification came, forty days after giving birth to Jesus, Mary and Joseph brought Him to the temple in Jerusalem. The Spirit enlightened Simeon to know when Jesus was consecrated to God at the temple. He knew Jesus was going to save both the Israelites and the Gentiles. Mary and Joseph marveled at Simeon's words, which gave them confirmation of the significance of Jesus, who was entrusted to them.

THOSE IN THE SYNAGOGUE AT NAZARETH MARVELED!

> *"'The Spirit of the Lord is upon me, because he has anointed me to*
> *proclaim good news to the poor. He has sent me to proclaim liberty to*
> *the captives and recovering of sight to the blind, to set at liberty those*
> *who are oppressed, to proclaim the year of the Lord's favor.' And he*
> *rolled up the scroll and gave it back to the attendant and sat down. And*
> *the eyes of all in the synagogue were fixed on him. And he began to say*
> *to them, 'Today this Scripture has been fulfilled in your hearing.' And*
> *all spoke well of him and **marveled** at the gracious words that were*
> *coming from his mouth. And they said, 'Is not this Joseph's son?'"*
> ~ Luke 4:18-22 (ESV)

Shortly after Jesus' public ministry began, He was preaching in Nazareth, the city He grew up in. He unrolled the scroll and read the first part of the passage above, which was from the book of Isaiah, revealing who He was. Those in the synagogue knew that Jesus was the son of Joseph, a carpenter, whom they did not regard as wise or important. They marveled that Jesus was speaking words of God's grace as He revealed that God's Spirit was upon Him.

Jesus' Disciples Marveled!

> *"One day he got into a boat with his disciples, and he said to them, 'Let us go across to the other side of the lake.' So they set out, and as they sailed he fell asleep. And a windstorm came down on the lake, and they were filling with water and were in danger. And they went and woke him, saying, 'Master, Master, we are perishing!' And he awoke and rebuked the wind and the raging waves, and they ceased, and there was calm. He said to them, 'Where is your faith?' And they were afraid, and they **marveled**, saying to one another, 'Who then is this, that he commands even winds and water, and they obey him?'"*
> ~ Luke 8:22-25 (ESV)

The disciples spent much time with Jesus as He taught them, and they saw the many miracles Jesus performed. Even with that first-hand knowledge, they became scared when a storm arose on the Sea of Galilee. They awoke Jesus to let Him know they were going to die. Jesus rebuked the sea and calmed the storm. The disciples were surprised to see how even the wind and storms were under Jesus' control. Despite being afraid, they marveled at Jesus' power.

Jesus Marveled!

> *"He went away from there and came to his hometown, and his disciples followed him. And on the Sabbath he began to teach in the synagogue, and many who heard him were astonished, saying, 'Where did this man get these things? What is the wisdom given to him? How are such mighty works done by his hands? Is not this the carpenter, the son of Mary and brother of James and Joses and Judas and Simon? And are not his sisters here with*

*us?' And they took offense at him. And Jesus said to them, 'A prophet is not without honor, except in his hometown and among his relatives and in his own household.' And he could do no mighty work there, except that he laid his hands on a few sick people and healed them. And he **marveled** because of their unbelief. And he went about among the villages teaching."*
~ Mark 6:1-6 (ESV)

Jesus returned to Nazareth and began teaching in the synagogue. The people marveled at the wisdom Jesus shared and the mighty deeds He performed. Sadly, they questioned if a carpenter's son could truly do the supernatural things they saw. Because of their lack of faith, Jesus had to leave the area. Jesus marveled at their lack of faith and moved on from Nazareth.

Once, when Jesus entered Capernaum, there was a centurion's servant who was sick and about to die. The centurion knew of Jesus and asked some elders to summon Jesus to heal his servant.

*"And Jesus went with them. When he was not far from the house, the centurion sent friends, saying to him, 'Lord, do not trouble yourself, for I am not worthy to have you come under my roof. Therefore I did not presume to come to you. But say the word, and let my servant be healed. For I too am a man set under authority, with soldiers under me: and I say to one, "Go," and he goes; and to another, "Come," and he comes; and to my servant, "Do this," and he does it.' When Jesus heard these things, he **marveled** at him, and turning to the crowd that followed him, said, 'I tell you, not even in Israel have I found such faith.'"*
~ Luke 7:6-9 (ESV)

The centurion showed genuine concern for his servant. He also displayed great faith, knowing that Jesus did not need to be physically present to heal his servant. Jesus marveled at his faith and even stated that He did not know of any person in Israel who had such faith. What an example the centurion gave us.

A FRIEND AND I MARVELED!

A friend read in a church bulletin about the need to visit homebound people. He felt an inkling that God was calling him to do it, but he didn't want to. As he went about his chores, the Lord kept prompting him to look at the bulletin again, impressing upon him to step out and call about this need. He finally said, "Yes, Lord." When he connected with the man he was assigned to, he marveled at God's divine encounter. They discovered they grew up in the same town, about ninety minutes away; they attended the same school, being a year apart, and were in the Army at the same time, reporting to the same colonel. With my friend saying "yes" to the Lord, he stepped out in faith, knowing God was working. We both marveled at how God brought them together after all those years.

When we are open to the Spirit, we can't help but marvel at what happens. Be encouraged to step out in faith.

Be encouraged to marvel at…

> how God's Word speaks to your life.
> the empty tomb.
> the salvation of the world and Jesus, the light to the Gentiles.
> the words of grace that Jesus speaks.
> the storms in your life that Jesus calms.
> the power of faith that causes supernatural events to occur.
> what miracles Jesus can do when you have faith.

Be encouraged to also be like the centurion in…

> recognizing the power of Jesus.
> knowing God is in control of everything.
> trusting God to guide and lead.

REFLECTION:

What have you marveled at about Jesus recently as you saw Him working in your life?

Does your faith make Jesus marvel?

"And the glory of the Lord will be revealed, and all people will see it together. For the mouth of the Lord has spoken."

~ Isaiah 40:5

67

Ministry Reflections

Ministry can take many forms. For some, it might be something formal in a church setting, such as a parish council, an elder in the church, a funeral committee, or an usher or greeter. But ministry encompasses much more than the traditional roles in the church.

I found this definition for ministry in a Google search: "a person or thing through which something is accomplished."

What if the thing accomplished is sharing the Jesus in you with others?

Sharing Him through the way you live,
        the activities you are busy with,
                and through your words.

Ministry can also be viewed as…

> caring for an aging parent.
> taking a neighbor to the store weekly.
> encouraging others through emails.
> volunteering at a hospital or other organization.
> being a handyman for someone who is wheelchair-bound.
> writing letters to shut-ins or to those in jail.
> making meals for people after surgery.
> posting inspirational thoughts on social media.

About two years ago, before officially joining a different church, I sent the deacon a link to the writing I had done about a Witness Walk he organized the year before. Much to my surprise, shortly after, he wanted to meet with me. The first thing he asked me was, "What do you see with your ministry?" I was surprised by his question because no one had ever mentioned my writings as a ministry before.

Since that meeting, God has shown me one ripple effect after another with this ministry. What started as a test to see if God would provide inspiration each week has indeed turned into a ministry. It is a ministry that first touches my heart and, for my benefit, helps me process how God is working all around me. What will God provide for inspiration this week, to touch my heart, of seeing Him working in the simple, ordinary things in life? How can I share Him through the written word? If one other person is touched in a given week, if they see something differently because of this ministry, it is an added blessing.

With any ministry we are involved in, there are lessons we can learn. In this writing ministry, I have learned...

> we need to step out in faith, trusting God.
> God can stretch us beyond what we think we can do.
> God sometimes puts people in our lives for specific purposes, possibly for just a season.
> we need to remain faithful to God while doing our part.
> God gets the glory for all ministry.
> we need to keep pursuing the gifts God has given us.
> our hearts are most important in ministry; the number of people who read is not important.

It is vital that we remember **who** produces the fruit in any ministry.

"What, after all, is Apollos? And what is Paul? Only servants, through whom you came to believe—as the Lord has assigned to each his task. I planted the seed, Apollos watered it, but God has been making it grow."
~ 1 Corinthians 3:5-6

God is the only one who can make the seed of our ministry grow. Our focus is on being faithful servants of God. In all of our ministries, the purpose is to testify to the gospel of God's grace.

Paul's thoughts are the perfect prayer for whatever ministry we are working in.

"But I do not account my life of any value nor as precious to myself,
if only I may finish my course and the ministry that I received from
the Lord Jesus, to testify to the gospel of the grace of God."
~ Acts 20:24 (ESV)

Keep ministering in Jesus' name, sharing the good news of God's grace.

REFLECTION:

What are some lessons you have learned in a ministry you are involved in? What unexpected fruit was produced in your life through a ministry involvement?

"For everything comes from him and exists by his power and is
intended for his glory. All glory to him forever! Amen."
~ Romans 11:36 (NLT)

68

Jesus' Presence

When have you experienced Jesus' presence in a special encounter?

What were you doing at the time?
> Where did it take place?

It was the ripple effect of God's goodness that I listened to a sermon online from a local church. The deacon's message gave me knowledge about something I had not considered before, and I was able to relate to similar experiences he shared. This prompted me to text the deacon to let him know I appreciated his message. He responded, "The next time we see each other, I will share with you a personal encounter I had with Jesus a few weeks ago." I smiled with excitement and wonder.

As his story goes, he was cutting and stacking wood while listening to music with his headphones on. As the song, *All I Ask of You* from Phantom of the Opera came on, for some reason, only the first two stanzas played. Though the song is a love song between two people, the lyrics are a perfect parallel to reflecting on Jesus' love for each one of us personally. As soon as the deacon heard that first line, he stopped stacking the wood, stood still, and was immediately immersed in Jesus' presence. He felt Jesus surround him, even embrace him, in pure unconditional love as he soaked up the few moments of the special encounter. Here are some of the lyrics he was listening to:

> No more talk of darkness,
> Forget these wide-eyed fears;
> I'm here, nothing can harm you.[3]

The lyrics reveal the truth that with Jesus...

> there is no darkness.
> we need not fear.
> nothing can harm us.
> we have His words that comfort and calm us.
>
> we are free.
> our tears are dried.
> we are never alone, as He is always beside us.
> we have Him to guard and guide our path.

"Even though I walk through the darkest valley, I will fear no evil,
for you are with me; your rod and your staff, they comfort me."
~ Psalm 23:4

Even in the darkest valley, the light of Jesus can be found. Because of Jesus, we should fear no evil, as nothing can truly harm us. Nothing separates us from the love of God and the victory we have in Jesus. God's Word brings us comfort, knowing He is in control.

"The Lord himself goes before you and will be with you; he will never
leave you nor forsake you. Do not be afraid; do not be discouraged."
~ Deuteronomy 31:8

What comfort we have in knowing God not only goes before us but is always with us. We have freedom because we know He never abandons us and is always guiding us. Sometimes we need to fight our feelings of being forsaken while standing on God's Word.

As the deacon was reading the lyrics to me, I was surprised when he read **my** name. (I actually thought he inserted it in the lyrics.) When I read the lyrics, I was touched even more. What are the chances the person God would have him share this story with would be named Christine, the same name as in the song?

Anywhere you go, let me go too,
Christine, that's all I ask of you.[4]

Tears streamed down my face. I closed my eyes, envisioning Jesus speaking directly to me as I was reassured of His presence in my life. Take a moment to reread that last line, inserting your name instead of "Christine." These words apply to all of us.

Jesus wants…

us to love Him completely.
our love for Him to last our entire lives.
to lead us from solitude to the fullness of life.

us to rely completely on Him.
us to know He is always beside us.
to accompany us everywhere.

"Jesus replied: 'Love the Lord your God with all your heart
and with all your soul and with all your mind.'"
~ Matthew 22:37

"And to know the love of Christ that surpasses knowledge,
that you may be filled with all the fullness of God."
~ Ephesians 3:19 (ESV)

Our first priority is to love God with all that we have—heart, soul, and mind. Loving God above all else is the greatest vocation we have. We experience the fullness of life when we experience Jesus' great love for us.

"We think you ought to know, dear brothers and sisters, about the
trouble we went through in the province of Asia. We were crushed and
overwhelmed beyond our ability to endure, and we thought we would

never live through it. In fact, we expected to die. But as a result, we stopped
relying on ourselves and learned to rely only on God, who raises the dead.
And he did rescue us from mortal danger, and he will rescue us again. We
have placed our confidence in him, and he will continue to rescue us."
~ 2 Corinthians 1:8-10 (NLT)

Paul shares the hardships they endured and how they realized that when they put their total trust in God and not in themselves, they were rescued. What a great comfort to know that we can completely rely on God as He is always beside and with us everywhere we go. Our God, Abba, is with us through all we endure. He works everything out for our good.

May you be encouraged to…

> leave fear behind, knowing nothing can harm you with God on your side.
> be free, knowing God is walking with you and guiding your path.
> spend your life loving God and knowing He is always with you.
> see what opportunities arise for you to experience Jesus' presence.
> share your experiences of Jesus with others.

We just never know when Jesus' presence will present itself in our lives, do we?

REFLECTION:

What unique experience did Jesus reveal His presence to you powerfully? Have you shared some of your experiences with other like-minded people to encourage them?

"His divine power has given us everything we need for a godly life through
our knowledge of him who called us by his own glory and goodness."
~ 2 Peter 1:3

69

True Friends

What attributes come to mind when you think of a true friend?

We can learn some attributes of a true friend from thinking about...

> the example Jesus gave us.
> our relationship with Him.
> our own friends who might mirror Christ to us.

Remember, too, that a friendship works both ways:

It is a blessing to have true friends,

> and we have the honor of being true friends to others.

A true friend is someone...

> who really cares what is happening in your life.
> who walks with you, whether you are hurting or happy.
> who listens to you with all their heart.
> who shares your ups and downs.
> who makes you smile and laugh.
> you can depend on to support you, especially in your struggles.
> you can talk with about anything and everything.
> who shares their faith with you to help you grow.
> who encourages you in your walk.
> who challenges you to be a better you.
> who understands what you are saying.
> who shows compassion when you need it most.

Christine M. Fisher

who prays with and for you.

who reaches out to you and forgets about their own needs.

I thank the Lord for His gift and example of being a true friend to us, and I thank Him for the special true friends He places in our lives.

REFLECTION:

What is a memorable time a true friend was present when you needed them most?

When have you been available for a friend in a dark time for them?

> *"And you know that we treated each of you as a father treats his*
> *own children. We pleaded with you, encouraged you, and urged*
> *you to live your lives in a way that God would consider worthy.*
> *For he called you to share in his Kingdom and glory."*
> ~ 1 Thessalonians 2:11-12 (NLT)

70

God's Promises

When we are going through difficult things in life, isn't it easy to get sidetracked, thinking God is not with us? Don't we lose sight of God working? Isn't it natural to want to avoid suffering and heartache?

We know we cannot avoid suffering and difficult times. It is a part of life, and none of us escape it. What we can do is check our perspective.

Are we relying on God's strength?
> Are we allowing God's Word to speak to our hearts?
> > Are we reminding ourselves of God's promises?

What are some of God's promises to us?

I Am With You Always.

> *"No one will be able to stand against you all the days*
> *of your life. As I was with Moses, so I will be with*
> *you; I will never leave you nor forsake you."*
> ~ Joshua 1:5

I Will Give You Rest.

> *"Then Jesus said, 'Come to me, all of you who are weary*
> *and carry heavy burdens, and I will give you rest.'"*
> ~ Matthew 11:28 (NLT)

Christine M. Fisher

I WILL TAKE CARE OF YOUR NEEDS.

> *"And my God will supply every need of yours according
> to his riches in glory in Christ Jesus."*
> ~ Philippians 4:19 (ESV)

I WILL GIVE YOU STRENGTH AND HELP.

> *"Don't be afraid, for I am with you. Don't be discouraged,
> for I am your God. I will strengthen you and help you. I
> will hold you up with my victorious right hand."*
> ~ Isaiah 41:10 (NLT)

I WILL WORK EVERYTHING OUT FOR YOUR GOOD.

> *"And we know that God causes everything to work together for the good
> of those who love God and are called according to his purpose for them."*
> ~ Romans 8:28 (NLT)

What is God's purpose for us?

> To glorify God with our lives.
> To know God's presence intimately.
> To know that God is always with us.

How can God use everything, even the bad, for our good?

> It might be in our poverty or pain where we see the face of God
> in the one who provides.
> In our time of deepest despair, we might encounter the true
> presence of God.
> At a time of a health crisis, we may experience the voice of God
> leading us.

Consider these truths from Romans 8:28:

> No matter how dire our circumstances, God is still sovereign.
> No matter what happens to us, we are still in God's providential care.
> We can have joy, even in hardship, because we know God is with us.
> Our hope is built on trust in God.

I was reminded of how God used something unpleasant for His good in my life. I was experiencing dental inflammation that had gotten quite painful. In the process of picking up a prescription, I saw a person I briefly knew and, through conversation, we decided to get together weekly to talk and study the Bible. Two days later, we met and enjoyed a spirit-filled conversation. God used the health issue I was experiencing to orchestrate His perfect timing to strike up another blessed encounter for His glory.

Take a few moments to ponder each of the following thoughts:

> Our hardest times often lead to our greatest moments.
> Things don't happen to us; things happen for us.
> God is stretching and growing us through our struggles and trials.
> God is always up to something.
> We are a work in progress, growing and improving each day.

How much peace do you experience in the trials of life? I think it is often a struggle, especially at first.

> *"On the evening of that first day of the week, when the disciples were together, with the doors locked for fear of the Jewish leaders, Jesus came and stood among them and said, 'Peace be with you!' After he said this, he showed them his hands and side. The disciples were overjoyed when they saw the Lord. Again Jesus said, 'Peace be*

Christine M. Fisher

with you! As the Father has sent me, I am sending you.' And with
that he breathed on them and said, 'Receive the Holy Spirit.'"
~ John 20:19-22

The first thing Jesus said to His disciples after His resurrection was *"peace."* He repeated it a second time. The disciples were afraid and fearful, yet Jesus reassured them that everything would be okay. Jesus sent them off to continue to share the good news, knowing the Holy Spirit would be with them.

This statement is a powerful thought:

> The amount of peace you have in life is equal to
> the amount of trust you have in God.

Isn't that a great truth? If we truly believe God is working everything out for our good and His purpose prevails in our lives, shouldn't we have that true peace? His peace surpasses all understanding. Don't we then trust God completely with everything that happens?

Let's work on having peace and trust in God as we go through the hardships of life.

Stay connected with God.

> Abiding in Christ more and more brings us to that place of peace. Be reminded that God is always working all the circumstances out in our lives for our good because of His great love for us.

REFLECTION:

What promise of God do you hold on to the most?
Can you see God working all things for His glory?

"What if God, although choosing to show his wrath and make his power known, bore with great patience the objects of his wrath—prepared for destruction? What if he did this to make the riches of his glory known to the objects of his mercy, whom he prepared in advance for glory—"
~ Romans 9:22-23

71

Our Supernatural God

We tend to live and view life focusing on things that relate to our five senses, and the way we perceive life through our senses affects and influences the way we see God working. Have you thought about how God calls us to see Him working using our spiritual senses?

SIGHT

What we can physically **see** with our eyes is what is usually our reality. Maybe God is calling us to develop spiritual eyes to see how He is constantly working, even if we do not physically see Him.

"Then Jesus told him, 'Because you have seen me, you have believed; blessed are those who have not seen and yet have believed.'"
~ John 20:29

SOUND

The things we can audibly **hear** with our ears from so many others are what we believe. Maybe God is calling us to develop spiritual ears to hear His voice alone—the only voice that matters.

"My sheep listen to my voice; I know them, and they follow me."
~ John 10:27

TASTE

The food we **taste** is what we seek more of. Maybe God is calling us to develop spiritual food to seek more of Him and taste how good He truly is.

> *"Taste and see that the Lord is good. Oh, the*
> *joys of those who take refuge in him!"*
> ~ Psalm 34:8 (NLT)

Touch

With the sense of **touch**, we can feel a gamut of emotions, from anger to happiness. Maybe God is calling us to develop a spiritual sense of His touch, with His compassion, in our lives.

> *"Moved with compassion, Jesus reached out and touched*
> *him. 'I am willing,' he said. 'Be healed!'"*
> ~ Mark 1:41 (NLT)

Smell

The aromas we can **smell** can influence our moods. Maybe God is calling us to develop a spiritual fragrance that is pleasing to Him.

> *"For we are to God the pleasing aroma of Christ among those*
> *who are being saved and those who are perishing."*
> ~ 2 Corinthians 2:15

Using our five senses influences our feelings and emotions. These feelings often factor into the way we feel about our relationship with God. If we tend to use our physical senses, we have more feelings of sadness, anger, or loneliness. If we use our spiritual senses, we experience more happiness and joy, which isn't as dependent on our circumstances.

God works beyond the visible, observable universe and transcends the laws of nature. It is important to develop our spiritual senses because God is a supernatural God at work. Merriam-Webster.com defines supernatural as:

Christine M. Fisher

1. of or relating to an order of existence beyond the visible, observable universe; especially of or relating to God or a god, demigod, spirit, or devil.

2a. departing from what is usual or normal especially so as to appear to transcend the laws of nature.

2b. attributed to an invisible agent (such as a ghost or spirit).

Consider these examples of God at work supernaturally.

God said, *"Let there be light"* (Genesis 1:3).

The way Jesus was conceived. It was not through human means but via the Holy Spirit—indeed, supernaturally (Matthew 1:18-21).

Jesus fed the five thousand with five barley loaves and two small fish (John 6:1-15).

The woman who had been bleeding for twelve years suddenly touched Jesus' cloak and was immediately healed (Luke 8:43-48).

Simon, James, and John were fishing all night and did not catch anything, Jesus came along and told them to put their nets down again. Their catch filled two boats with fish (Luke 5:1-11).

Jesus and Peter walked on the water (Matthew 14:22-36).

Jesus raised Lazarus from the dead after being dead for four days (John 11:38-44).

Jesus died and was then resurrected (Luke 24:1-12).

Since God says, *"I, the Lord, do not change"* (Malachi 3:6), God still works supernaturally today. You ask, "In what ways?"

That time, you…

> received a text from someone saying they were praying for you at
> the moment you needed it the most.
> just happened to bump into an old friend who ended up needing
> your friendship which blessed them.
> met that person who became a Christian mentor in your life.
> saw that special sign that reminded you of a loved one.
> received a note of encouragement just when you were about to
> give up.
> were healed from cancer.

Try exercising your spiritual senses and see the many ways God is
supernaturally at work in your life.

REFLECTION:

What supernatural act did God perform in your life?
Who has shared a miracle in their life with you?

> *"And I pray that he would unveil within you the unlimited riches*
> *of his glory and favor until supernatural strength floods your*
> *innermost being with his divine might and explosive power."*
> ~ Ephesians 3:16 (TPT)

72

Easter Joy

Easter is a joyful time
　　when we see God's love at its fullest.
　　　　Life is beginning anew.

If we look around, we see God's love unfolding in nature—
　　the trees begin to blossom
　　　　and the chirping of the birds can be heard.
　　　　Life is beginning anew.

Easter is when God sent His only Son, Jesus Christ,
　　to die for you and me
　　　　and then to rise on the third day.
　　　　Life is beginning anew.

We are God's creation,
　　and Jesus' love must be reflected in each of us.
　　　　The Lord loved you so much that He died for you.
　　　　Life is beginning anew.

Let us share that Easter joy of the resurrection
　　with every person we encounter
　　　　and enrich their lives with our presence
　　　　　　because of what Jesus did for us!
　　　　Life is beginning anew.

REFLECTION:

How have you experienced Easter joy in your life?
What new beginning in life do you find inspiring?

> *"Arise, shine, for your light has come, and the*
> *glory of the Lord rises upon you."*
> ~ Isaiah 60:1

73

Postures of Worship

As Christians, we have the privilege and responsibility of worshiping God above all else. Our postures of worship are ways we give glory to God. From the following definition, we learn worship should only be rendered to God and God alone.

The KJV Dictionary definition of worship is: "homage rendered to God, which it is sinful (idolatry) to render to any created being."

> *"Jesus answered, 'It is written: "Worship the*
> *Lord your God and serve him only."'"*
> ~ Luke 4:8

Jesus instructed and modeled for us to worship and serve only God in and with our lives. Everything He did was to worship and serve God.

> *"The Lord says: 'These people come near to me with their mouth and*
> *honor me with their lips, but their hearts are far from me. Their worship*
> *of me is based on merely human rules they have been taught.'"*
> ~ Isaiah 29:13

Our worship reflects what is in our hearts. If we worship God because we feel obligated, it is not true worship. True worship comes from our love and respect for who God is.

Hearing an interesting sermon made me reflect on the different postures of worship and their significance.

The four main postures of worship are:

> Standing
> Sitting
> Kneeling
> Prostrating

What is the significance of each posture, what Scripture passages reference them, and how can they help us through the storms of life?

STANDING

When we stand and worship, we get a sense of community or oneness with the Lord, indicating honor and reverence for Him. If we worship with our arms outstretched, we express our openness to receiving God's blessings. We welcome His Spirit to fill us with His presence. We expose our true selves to God.

> *"A large crowd soon gathered around him, so he got into a boat.*
> *Then he sat there and taught as the people stood on the shore."*
> ~ Matthew 13:2 (NLT)

> *"And there will be strange signs in the sun, moon, and stars. And here on*
> *earth the nations will be in turmoil, perplexed by the roaring seas and*
> *strange tides. People will be terrified at what they see coming upon the earth,*
> *for the powers in the heavens will be shaken. Then everyone will see the Son*
> *of Man coming on a cloud with power and great glory. So when all these*
> *things begin to happen, stand and look up, for your salvation is near!"*
> ~ Luke 21:25-28 (NLT)

Crowds of people came to hear Jesus speak as they stood on the seashore. Jesus tells us to stand tall and look up to see the Son of Man, even when terrible events are surrounding us. Raise your head and look up.

In the storms of life, when we stand in God's presence with our hands raised in praise of Him, He fills us with His love and peace. We need to be aware of seeing God, His goodness, and His beauty in all circumstances.

SITTING

When we worship in the sitting posture, we are most often listening to, reading, or observing God and His word. It is important to sit, be still, and spend time in His presence.

> *"She (Martha) had a sister called Mary, who sat at the Lord's feet listening to what he said."*
> ~ Luke 10:39

> *"From Perga they* [Paul and Barnabas] *went on to Pisidian Antioch. On the Sabbath they entered the synagogue and sat down. After the reading from the Law and the Prophets, the leaders of the synagogue sent word to them, saying, 'Brothers, if you have a word of exhortation for the people, please speak.'"*
> ~ Acts 13:14-15

Mary, the sister of Lazarus and Martha, was the perfect example of someone who knew the importance of sitting and listening to Jesus. She did not let distractions get in the way. Paul and Barnabas also knew they needed to hear the Word of God so they could share it with others.

In the storms of life, we need to take time to sit and read God's Word, meditating on the lessons Jesus shared and applying them to our lives. The Word brings us comfort in times of distress.

KNEELING

Kneeling to worship is a respectful and reverent position. It is prayerful and often accompanied by closing the eyes and, sometimes, folding the hands. It is one of acknowledging that God is over everything in heaven and earth.

> *"Come, let us bow down in worship, let us kneel before*
> *the Lord our Maker; for he is our God and we are the*
> *people of his pasture, the flock under his care…"*
> ~ Psalm 95:6-7

> *"For this reason I [Paul] kneel before the Father, from whom every family*
> *in heaven and on earth derives its name. I pray that out of his glorious*
> *riches he may strengthen you with power through his Spirit in your*
> *inner being, so that Christ may dwell in your hearts through faith…"*
> ~ Ephesians 3:14-17

We confess submission to the Lord by kneeling before Him. When we kneel, it helps us remember that God is our shepherd, who cares for us. God, as the Creator of all, deserves our reverence. Paul recognized the importance of kneeling before God as he was praying in earnest for the people of Ephesus.

In the storms of life, taking time to worship the Lord by kneeling and praying for His intercession is vital. It helps us remember that God is supreme and works everything out for our good.

PROSTRATING

Prostrating oneself in worship of God reflects absolute surrender and humility. I believe it qualifies as the ultimate form of worship. We are willing to submit ourselves totally to God and His perfect will.

> *"While Jesus was in one of the towns, a man came along who was*
> *covered with leprosy. When he saw Jesus, he fell with his face to the*
> *ground and begged him, 'Lord, if you are willing, you can make*

me clean.' Jesus reached out his hand and touched the man. 'I am
willing,' he said. 'Be clean!' And immediately the leprosy left him."
~ Luke 5:12-13

"Then Jesus went with his disciples to a place called Gethsemane, and he
said to them, 'Sit here while I go over there and pray.' He took Peter and
the two sons of Zebedee along with him, and he began to be sorrowful
and troubled. Then he said to them, 'My soul is overwhelmed with sorrow
to the point of death. Stay here and keep watch with me.' Going a little
farther, he fell with his face to the ground and prayed, 'My Father, if it is
possible, may this cup be taken from me. Yet not as I will, but as you will.'"
~ Matthew 26:36-39

The man with leprosy was ready to surrender his life to Jesus. He knew Jesus had the power to heal his leprosy. Jesus knew the leper's heart was ready to accept Him and His power.

Jesus gave us the ultimate example of absolute surrender and humility to God's will when asking God one more time if the cup of suffering, death on a cross, could be taken away. He prostrated Himself in surrender to God's ultimate will.

In the storms of life, we might prostrate ourselves, being overcome with despair and begging God to answer our prayers favorably. To prostrate ourselves just as Jesus did is a great way to show God that we surrender to His will no matter what. We humble ourselves before our Father.

One Good Friday, my pastor and deacon prostrated themselves before the cross in humble adoration of Jesus' sacrifice for each of us. I, too, wanted to experience that, so one day after service, when the church was empty, I prostrated myself under the crucifix. It was a humbling, meaningful time of surrendering my life once again to God and thanking Jesus for dying for my sins.

May you take time to reflect on worship in your life.

> Be reminded that there are many different postures of worship, and there is no one way that is correct.

>> Keep worshiping and glorifying the Lord, for He is worthy of our praise.

REFLECTION:

Are you encouraged to explore a new posture of worship?
What is the most powerful time of worship you have experienced?

> *"All the nations you have made shall come and worship*
> *before you, O Lord, and shall glorify your name."*
> ~ Psalm 86:9 (ESV)

74

God's Breath

Though we can't see the wind, we see its effects and how it is under God's command. Biblically, the wind, when positively portrayed, is symbolic of the Holy Spirit. Just like the wind, one cannot usually see breath, yet God uses it powerfully for His purposes.

What does Scripture tell us about breath?

> *"Then the Lord God formed the man from the dust of the ground. He breathed the breath of life into the man's nostrils, and the man became a living person."*
> ~ Genesis 2:7 (NLT)

God decided to create man in His image to rule over all the creatures. To do this, God, like a potter, formed man from the dust of the ground. The way God brought man to life was to breathe His very breath of life into man's nostrils. We, as humans, made in God's image, have the Spirit of God breathed into us. What a powerful thought to see God's goodness.

> *"On the evening of that day, the first day of the week, the doors being locked where the disciples were for fear of the Jews, Jesus came and stood among them and said to them, 'Peace be with you.' When he had said this, he showed them his hands and his side. Then the disciples were glad when they saw the Lord. Jesus said to them again, 'Peace be with you. As the Father has sent me, even so I am sending you.' And when he had said this, he breathed on them and said to*

them, 'Receive the Holy Spirit. If you forgive the sins of any, they are forgiven them; if you withhold forgiveness from any, it is withheld.'"
~ John 20:19-23 (ESV)

This powerful encounter was the first time the resurrected Jesus appeared to His disciples. They were hiding, afraid of what happened to Jesus, and fearing for their lives. The first thing that Jesus wanted to impart to the disciples was peace. He didn't want them to be afraid, but to have the peace that surpasses all understanding. His message was one of sending them into the world to preach the good news of Jesus.

Jesus' breathing on the disciples was a breath of fresh air in their lives, which brought forth the Holy Spirit in a new, more powerful way. No longer were they fearful; they were filled with courage, wisdom, knowledge, and the power to heal.

Just as Jesus was on the journey with His disciples, we need to remember, too, that Jesus is with us every step of the way. As disciples of Jesus, we have the breath of God and the Holy Spirit in our lives. We have the power to live in the Spirit as courageous disciples.

When the winds of life come with gale-force strength, we need to hold onto Jesus, our anchor. Relief comes through faith.

It is an acceptance that
>> the wind always changes direction
>>> when we learn to accept
>>>> the breath of the Holy Spirit
>>>>> in our lives.

Be encouraged to experience and know that...

God is breathing His breath of life into you daily.

Christine M. Fisher

Jesus is breathing the Holy Spirit afresh on you, giving new life to your spirit.

the Holy Spirit in you dispels fear and fills you with courage.

your breath of life is like the wind as you share the Holy Spirit that is in you.

REFLECTION:

How has God breathed life into your spirit?

Do you pray for an outpouring of the Spirit in your life?

"So all of us who have had that veil removed can see and reflect the glory of the Lord. And the Lord—who is the Spirit—makes us more and more like him as we are changed into his glorious image."
~ 2 Corinthians 3:18 (NLT)

75

The Light

One day I had a little revelation as the sun was shining through my window.

The sun represents Jesus, the Son. The crosses visible in the window represent our lives. Notice there are two crosses joined, showing our connectedness. Our lives, filled with Jesus' light, are radiant and keep the ripple effect of His light shining for others. The original cross became the shadow of a new cross. Our lives become light for others, and we keep the light of Christ going. Our shining light makes shadows in the lives of the people we meet.

"Again Jesus spoke to them, saying, 'I am the light of the world. Whoever follows me will not walk in darkness, but will have the light of life.'"
~ John 8:12 (ESV)

"You are the light of the world. A city set on a hill cannot be hidden. Nor do people light a lamp and put it under a basket, but on a stand, and it gives light to all in the house."
~ Matthew 5:14-15 (ESV)

We have the assurance that, as we follow Jesus, the light of the world, we too will have the light of life in us. Our light is to shine brightly, just as Jesus did. When we have light, we cannot hide it. It shines into the lives of all those we meet.

"Those who live in the shelter of the Most High will find rest in the shadow of the Almighty. This I declare about the Lord: He alone is my refuge, my place of safety; he is my God, and I trust him."
~ Psalm 91:1-2 (NLT)

As we live moment by moment with God, the Most High, our souls find rest in His shadow. We are well cared for and protected in His shadow, no matter what happens. God is with us through the good and the bad. He is our God, and we can trust Him. His love, care, and protection are with us all the time.

My inspiration for you is to…

> let Jesus fill you with His light.
> take Jesus' light and let it shine brightly, filling the lives of the people you meet.
> know in God's shadow, His love, care, and protection are with you.
> find rest in the shadow.

REFLECTION:

What reminds you of God's light shining in you?
What is one way you shine God's light?

> *"No longer will you need the sun to shine by day, nor the moon to give its light by night, for the Lord your God will be your everlasting light, and your God will be your glory."*
> ~ Isaiah 60:19 (NLT)

76

Foot Washing

"It was just before the Passover Festival. Jesus knew that the hour
had come for him to leave this world and go to the Father. Having
loved his own who were in the world, he loved them to the end. The
evening meal was in progress, and the devil had already prompted
Judas, the son of Simon Iscariot, to betray Jesus. Jesus knew that the
Father had put all things under his power, and that he had come
from God and was returning to God; so he got up from the meal, took
off his outer clothing, and wrapped a towel around his waist. After
that, he poured water into a basin and began to wash his disciples'
feet, drying them with the towel that was wrapped around him.

"He came to Simon Peter, who said to him, 'Lord, are you going
to wash my feet?' Jesus replied, 'You do not realize now what I am
doing, but later you will understand.' 'No,' said Peter, 'you shall never
wash my feet.' Jesus answered, 'Unless I wash you, you have no part
with me.' 'Then, Lord,' Simon Peter replied, 'not just my feet but my
hands and my head as well!' Jesus answered, 'Those who have had a
bath need only to wash their feet; their whole body is clean. And you
are clean, though not every one of you.' For he knew who was going
to betray him, and that was why he said not everyone was clean.

"When he had finished washing their feet, he put on his clothes and
returned to his place. 'Do you understand what I have done for you?' he
asked them. 'You call me "Teacher" and "Lord," and rightly so, for that is
what I am. Now that I, your Lord and Teacher, have washed your feet,
you also should wash one another's feet. I have set you an example that

you should do as I have done for you. Very truly I tell you, no servant is
greater than his master, nor is a messenger greater than the one who sent
him. Now that you know these things, you will be blessed if you do them.'"
~ John 13:1-17

When a worship service has a foot washing event, I want to participate in it. I know people usually prefer not to. I find it an honor to put myself in Jesus' presence as a disciple and visualize Him serving me personally because of His great love for me.

Why did Jesus wash His disciples' feet?

To...

> show His great love for them.
> demonstrate being a humble servant.
> symbolize our need for spiritual cleansing.
> set forth the principle of selfless service that would be exemplified on the cross.
> show us what we are to do for others.

I never considered the reason "to symbolize our need for spiritual cleansing" with Jesus' response to Peter, saying, *"Unless I wash you, you have no part with me."* Jesus' words go beyond the external washing of the disciples' feet. This is symbolic of spiritual cleansing. This comes from the cleansing in the waters of baptism as well as the cleansing of Jesus' blood shed for us. Ultimately, Peter, like us, needed both spiritual cleansings from Jesus.

"This is the one who came by water and blood—Jesus Christ.
He did not come by water only, but by water and blood. And it
is the Spirit who testifies, because the Spirit is the truth."
~ 1 John 5:6

Jesus knew at the foot washing that His time to walk in obedience to God's plan of salvation was quickly approaching. He was preparing His disciples for life without Him and teaching them to carry out the mission He began. A spiritual cleansing was necessary in their ministry, just as Jesus experienced. Jesus' public ministry began with John, His cousin, baptizing Him in the Jordan River, and ended with His crucifixion on the cross.

> *"Now that I, your Lord and Teacher, have washed your feet,*
> *you also should wash one another's feet. I have set you an*
> *example that you should do as I have done for you."*
> ~ John 13:14-15

Jesus was calling His disciples to follow His example of washing others' feet. That is why Jesus gave us the example and told us that we, too, would be blessed if we walk in obedience.

How is God calling you to wash others' feet?

By…

> having you pray for and love the person who has hurt you?
> bringing some necessities to the homeless person you see on the street?
> sharing the gospel with someone who does not know the Lord?
> giving of your time or talent to help someone who is in need?

I wrote these thoughts before going to a foot washing event. Often, I see people only putting one foot into the basin to be washed. We know Jesus washed both of His disciples' feet so, when it was my turn, I slipped both feet into the bowl. It was a sacred encounter when, while washing my feet, the person looked into my eyes and smiled, reflecting the love of Christ. The person then cupped his hands around my feet as he wrapped the towel around them and kissed one foot. I experienced Jesus' love embracing me through the holding of my feet. I felt complete and immersed in oneness with the Lord as I closed my eyes and listened to the beautiful music being sung. It was a sacred moment with the Lord.

Be encouraged to see how you can live out...

> loving others with Jesus' unconditional love.
> how Jesus is calling you to be a humble servant.
> receiving Jesus' spiritual cleansing of water and His blood.
> following Jesus' principle of selfless service to others.
> following Jesus' example of foot washing in others' lives.

REFLECTION:

What is one way you have lived out washing someone's feet?
Have you experienced Jesus washing your feet?

> *"And he said to me, 'You are my servant, Israel,*
> *in whom I will be glorified.'"*
> ~ Isaiah 49:3 (ESV)

77

Martha or Mary

"As Jesus and his disciples were on their way, he came to a village where a woman named Martha opened her home to him. She had a sister called Mary, who sat at the Lord's feet listening to what he said. But Martha was distracted by all the preparations that had to be made. She came to him and asked, 'Lord, don't you care that my sister has left me to do the work by myself? Tell her to help me!' 'Martha, Martha,' the Lord answered, 'you are worried and upset about many things, but few things are needed—or indeed only one. Mary has chosen what is better, and it will not be taken away from her.'"
~ Luke 10:38-42

What lessons might we incorporate into our daily lives by looking at Martha and Mary and what Jesus said about them?

MARTHA...

> opened her home to the Lord.
> was distracted with preparations.
> was worried and upset about many things.
> approached Jesus to ask if He cared that Mary was not helping.
> wanted Jesus to tell Mary to help with the preparations.
> thought Mary should be busy doing the same things as she was around the house.

MARY...

> did not busy herself with doing things around the house.

sat at the Lord's feet.

listened to what Jesus was saying.

Isn't it interesting that Jesus said to Martha:

> *"but few things are needed—or indeed only one. Mary has chosen*
> *what is better, and it will not be taken away from her."*
> ~ Luke 10:42

I am definitely a Martha as far as trying to **do** things, especially in the home. There always seem to be other priorities to be done.

Working

Grocery shopping

Planning and coordinating of schedules

Dishes

Cleaning

Paperwork

Bills to pay

Running children to different events and also attending them

Planning and making meals

Volunteer work

and the list goes on and on.

It seems if I'm not **doing**, I'm not being useful or productive. Reflecting on this story is a great thing to remember that finding ways to listen and spend time with Jesus is most important.

We can do this through…

prayer, which can really be done anywhere, at any time.

reading Scripture.

attending retreats and seminars.

small group sharing.

Bible studies.

visiting the sick, lonely, or poor.

writing to inspire others in their walk with the Lord.

sharing with other Christian friends who can encourage and inspire us.

listening to inspiring worship music.

I think the challenge is to be like both Martha and Mary and to keep that **balance** in our lives. What a great story to remind us of who and what are most important.

REFLECTION:

Do you have to make a conscious effort to be more like Martha or Mary? What is your favorite way to spend time with Jesus?

> *"If you remain in me and my words remain in you, ask whatever you wish, and it will be done for you. This is to my Father's glory, that you bear much fruit, showing yourselves to be my disciples."*
> ~ John 15:7-8

78

Time to Be With Him

I have had the privilege of joining a weekly Zoom Bible study, which is hosted in Wales by a pastor-friend. This Bible study is in a different format than other Bible studies I have participated in, which has made the Scriptures come to life. There are no formal study guides or homework for the next week. We usually read one chapter a week and then discuss the stories, their significance, and how God speaks to us through His words. I appreciate learning from the in-depth discussion of the passages as the pastor shares insightful wisdom.

When we read through Mark's gospel, there was one verse in particular that serves as great encouragement for our lives; this verse is only found in Mark's gospel account of Jesus appointing the twelve disciples.

> *"Jesus went up on a mountainside and called to him those he wanted, and they came to him.* **He appointed twelve that they might be with him and that he might send them out to preach and to have authority to drive out demons.** *These are the twelve he appointed: Simon (to whom he gave the name Peter), James son of Zebedee and his brother John (to them he gave the name Boanerges, which means 'sons of thunder'), Andrew, Philip, Bartholomew, Matthew, Thomas, James son of Alphaeus, Thaddaeus, Simon the Zealot and Judas Iscariot, who betrayed him."*
> ~ Mark 3:13-19

Jesus was thirty years old when He started His public ministry. Early on, Jesus appointed the twelve men listed above to be more intimately involved in proclaiming the good news to all.

Notice the three things Jesus mentions for the apostles He called:

> That they might be with Him.
>> That He might send them out to preach.
>>> That they have authority to drive out demons.

The first thing Jesus wants His newly appointed apostles to do is to be with Him. Jesus wanted a personal relationship with His apostles to be the most important thing. He wanted to get to know them and for them to truly know and understand Him.

That is precisely what Jesus wants for each of us. He wants a personal relationship with us above all else, which is the first priority in our faith walk. By spending time in prayer, reading Scripture, and seeing God working in our lives, we get to know Him better and understand His heart.

From that personal relationship with Jesus, the apostles were able to go out and preach, to share the good news of Jesus. The same is true of our relationship. As we nurture our personal relationship with Jesus, we are called to preach the good news in whatever way Jesus has gifted us, right where we are in our lives.

Mark's gospel starts with stories of Jesus' power over evil spirits and demons, showing that Jesus is indeed the Son of God. Jesus sent His first apostles out with that same power to even drive out demons. As the apostles watched in astonishment at Jesus doing this, they were even more amazed to be given the same power and authority.

Isn't the same principle true in our lives? God gives us the strength and power to do unimaginable things in our ministries. God alone gets the credit for whatever He does through us.

Jesus picked simple, ordinary men to be His first apostles. Most of them were fishermen, not teachers of the law or men in prominent positions of authority. Even Jesus came as a simple, ordinary man, not as a king, like people expected.

Aren't we simple, ordinary people, too, just like the earliest apostles? Jesus can use the simplest of us, with no formal education necessary. We only need to have a willing heart, be ready to serve, and share Jesus' love with all we meet. As the saying goes, "When God calls us, He will qualify us."

Have you considered how we are called human beings, not human doings? Isn't that what Jesus' life exemplified? Jesus did perform many miracles, but most important in His life was taking daily time to commune and pray with God, His Father. Many passages share that Jesus went to a mountain or off by Himself to pray. He was always seeking to be obedient to God, making sure to fulfill His purpose on earth.

We are called to just be with God every moment of every day. Don't think your doing is more important than just being. We, too, need to spend daily time in prayer and be obedient to God as we fulfill our life purpose on earth.

Take time daily to just be with Jesus.

Can you find a special place in your home or in nature where you can commune in prayer and Scripture with Him?

Can you try ten minutes a day and eventually work up to more? You will be surprised at how fast the time will go.

May Jesus minister to your heart and soul as you take time to be with Him, drawing you closer to Him.

REFLECTION:

Where do you go to just be with Jesus?
How does Jesus call you to preach about Him?

> *"God's glory is all around me! His wraparound presence is all I need,*
> *for the Lord is my Savior, my hero, and my life-giving strength. Trust*
> *only in God every moment! Tell him all your troubles and pour out your*
> *heart-longings to him. Believe me when I tell you—he will help you!"*
> ~ Psalm 62:7-8 (TPT)

79

Praise to Him

All glory and praise
Belong to our Lord,
Whose love has done more
Than we can afford.

Because of Jesus,
We can face each day
With love and peace
To brighten our way.

Since living with Him,
Life is easier to bear
Because we know
He's always there.

His greatest deed
Is hard to measure—
For eternity with Him
Is a priceless treasure.

REFLECTION:

Do you give glory and praise to God for His great love?
Have you thanked God for the priceless treasure of eternity with Him?

Christine M. Fisher

"No matter what, I'll trust in you to help me. Nothing will stop me from praising you to magnify your glory! I couldn't begin to count the times you've been there for me. With the skill of a poet, I'll never run out of things to say about how you faithfully kept me from danger."
~ Psalm 71:14-15 (TPT)

80

The Gift of Presence

Isn't Christmas a wonderful time of year when we take time to reflect on the sacredness of Jesus' birth? Christmas is also a time when we show our love to others, especially with the tradition of giving gifts. Have you stopped to think about what our gifts to one another symbolize?

Gifts are tangible symbols that say...

> you are important to me.
> I want to be in a relationship with you.
> I value you.
> I want you to be part of my life.

What is the best gift we have ever received?

> Hint: It might be intangible for now, but someday it will be tangible.

JESUS!

> Who gave us the gift of Jesus?

GOD!

> By giving us the ultimate gift of Jesus, God is saying to us...

> > you are important to me!
> > I want to be in a relationship with you!
> > I value you!
> > I want you to be part of my life!

"For God so loved the world that he gave his one and only Son, that whoever believes in him shall not perish but have eternal life."
~ John 3:16

God desires a personal relationship with us that begins here and will continue for eternity if we accept His gift of Jesus. How great God's love is for us.

"So God created mankind in his own image, in the image of God he created them; male and female he created them."
~ Genesis 1:27

God, the Creator of everything, made you and me in His image. He values each one of us. Reflect on the profound impact of that truth.

Have you accepted and opened your heart to Jesus, God's ultimate gift? When you receive God's gift of Jesus, your life is graced with Jesus' presence.

What can you give back to God for His gift of Jesus? How about in gratitude, sharing the presence of Jesus with others?

You can be Jesus to others by sharing…

> a loving heart.
> compassion for all of creation.
> forgiveness to those who have hurt you.
> grace in trying to understand another's view.
> the joy of the Lord.

"Shouldn't you have had mercy on your fellow servant just as I had on you?"
~ Matthew 18:33

God shows us mercy and compassion, most importantly by sending Jesus to save us from our sin. We need to share that same mercy and compassion with those who need a helping hand, someone to care about them, or are trying to find their way.

"Be kind and compassionate to one another, forgiving
each other, just as in Christ God forgave you."
~ Ephesians 4:32

We can learn from Christ, who was obedient to the point of death, even forgiving those who killed Him. Can you step out and forgive the one who has hurt you deeply?

When you share gifts with others, you share the presence of Jesus.

It also shows gratitude to God, letting Him know…

He is important to you.
you want to be in a relationship with Him.
you value Him.
you want Him to be part of your life.

God's gift of Jesus is the gift that keeps on giving.

"The abiding presence of that gift remains with us still;
the ongoing present is the ongoing presence of Jesus.
The real meaning of Christmas is presence—
the abiding presence of the One whose birth we celebrate this Christmas.
When you see the baby Jesus in the manger this Christmas,
see the visible, tangible sign of God's ardent desire
to be in relationship with you…
to affirm your value,
your importance in His eyes,

Christine M. Fisher

and God's wish to share in your life,
that you might share in His.
And then it is up to you…to go, and do likewise."
~ Fr. Michael Galuppi

"In the end, it is the reality of personal relationship that saves everything."
~ Thomas Merton

REFLECTION:

Do you know deep in your heart how special you are to God and Jesus? Have you experienced how Jesus is the greatest gift that keeps on giving in your life?

"The Word became flesh and made his dwelling among us.
We have seen his glory, the glory of the one and only Son,
who came from the Father, full of grace and truth."
~ John 1:14

81

The Body of Christ

A friend and I shared a few thoughts about the body of Christ that made me reflect more on that phrase and what it means in our lives.

Who is the head of the body of Christ? The One who was before everything in this world.

"Christ is the visible image of the invisible God. He existed before anything was created and is supreme over all creation, for through him God created everything in the heavenly realms and on earth. He made the things we can see and the things we can't see—such as thrones, kingdoms, rulers, and authorities in the unseen world. Everything was created through him and for him. He existed before anything else, and he holds all creation together. Christ is also the head of the church, which is his body. He is the beginning, supreme over all who rise from the dead. So he is first in everything."
~ Colossians 1:15-18 (NLT)

Who are the members of the body of Christ? We who believe in Jesus as our Lord and Savior.

"And now you Gentiles have also heard the truth, the Good News that God saves you. And when you believed in Christ, he identified you as his own by giving you the Holy Spirit, whom he promised long ago."
~ Ephesians 1:13 (NLT)

Christ, though He existed before all of creation, became the visible image of God in human form when He walked on this earth. Through Jesus, everything was created and came into being. That includes you and me.

Christine M. Fisher

Christ is the head of the church, which is His body. The members of the body of Christ are those who have heard the good news and put their faith in Jesus as their Savior. They become filled with the Holy Spirit. The church is not a physical building but consists of living people. Christ is supreme over everything because He was raised from the dead, the first of many.

There is only one head—Christ Himself. We are united with Christ because there is only one body and one Spirit.

> *"Make every effort to keep yourselves united in the Spirit, binding yourselves together with peace. For there is one body and one Spirit, just as you have been called to one glorious hope for the future."*
> ~ Ephesians 4:3-4 (NLT)

Christ, as the head, has all authority. The head directs the body.

> *"Jesus came and told his disciples, 'I have been given all authority in heaven and on earth.'"*
> ~ Matthew 28:18 (NLT)

We continue the mission of Christ since we are members of the body of Christ.

> *"Therefore go and make disciples of all nations, baptizing them in the name of the Father and of the Son and of the Holy Spirit, and teaching them to obey everything I have commanded you. And surely I am with you always, to the very end of the age."*
> ~ Matthew 28:19-20

The head consists of eyes to see God at work, ears to hear the Word of God, the mouth to proclaim the good news to others, and the nose to smell the fragrant aroma of God in this world. Christ, as the head, reflects these things to the other members of the body so we, in turn, can share Him through our lives.

What do we know about the members of the body of Christ?

"As it is, there are many parts, but one body."
~ 1 Corinthians 12:20

"Now you are the body of Christ, and each one of you is a part of it."
~ 1 Corinthians 12:27

"Just as our bodies have many parts and each part has a special function, so it is with Christ's body. We are many parts of one body, and we all belong to each other."
~ Romans 12:4-5 (NLT)

Just as our human bodies are made up of many parts, so is the body of Christ, which has many members, and each member has a special function. Our mission should be to fulfill the role God has gifted us with for the good of the body. We are united with Christ and the whole body. Being a member of the body of Christ is the highest calling of membership we have.

What should our lives look like as members of the body of Christ?

"This makes for harmony among the members, so that all the members care for each other. If one part suffers, all the parts suffer with it, and if one part is honored, all the parts are glad."
~ 1 Corinthians 12:25-26 (NLT)

"Instead, we will speak the truth in love, growing in every way more and more like Christ, who is the head of his body, the church. He makes the whole body fit together perfectly. As each

part does its own special work, it helps the other parts grow, so
that the whole body is healthy and growing and full of love."
~ Ephesians 4:15-16 (NLT)

As the body of Christ, our lives should reflect…

> harmony.
> showing we care.
> supporting those suffering.
> rejoicing in the positives.
> speaking the truth in love.
> growing to be more Christ-like.
> helping others grow in healthy ways.
> growing in and spreading Christ's love.

If we love Christ, the head of the body, we, too, love all the church, the members of the body.

My conversation with my friend included thoughts on how we don't necessarily feel comfortable sharing prayer requests with many members of the body of Christ.

Why does this so often happen in our lives? Sometimes we let our pride get in the way.

We feel misunderstood.
> We don't feel respected.
>> We are afraid to be vulnerable.
>>> We are too scared.
>>>> We fear judgment.

May you be encouraged to…

> reflect on your life as a member of the body of Christ.
> strive to make other members comfortable sharing their hearts and prayer needs with you.
> take a step towards asking a member of the body of Christ to pray for you.

REFLECTION:

What is one of your roles in the body of Christ?
When was the last time you asked someone to pray for you?

> *"I am in them and you are in me. May they experience such perfect unity that the world will know that you sent me and that you love them as much as you love me. Father, I want these whom you have given me to be with me where I am. Then they can see all the glory you gave me because you loved me even before the world began!"*
> ~ John 17:23-24 (NLT)

82

Tragedies

Do you sometimes question what God is doing in your life, especially when tragedies come along? Do you cry out to God, asking, "Why are you doing this to me?"

The book of Job shares insights into a good way to view and handle tragedies in our lives. The forty-two chapters of the book share the story of a wealthy, upright, and faithful man, Job. Satan, the accuser, was roaming the earth, seeking whomever he could destroy.

> *"Then the Lord asked Satan, 'Have you noticed my servant Job? He is the finest man in all earth. He is blameless—a man of complete integrity. He fears God and stays away from evil. And he has maintained his integrity, even though you urged me to harm him without cause.' Satan replied to the Lord, 'Skin for skin! A man will give up everything he has to save his life. But reach out and take away his health, and he will surely curse you to your face!' 'All right, do with him as you please,' the Lord said to Satan. 'But spare his life.'"*
> ~ Job 2:3-6 (NLT)

We learn Job lived a blameless, holy life and had much respect for God. His life embodied integrity. Satan was sure he could get Job to curse God if he sent tragedy into his life. God had faith in Job, and His only boundary was that Satan could not take Job's life.

Job owned a large number of oxen, donkeys, sheep, camels, and servants. They all perished tragically through attacks, lightning strikes, and a tornado, and all of his children died.

"Job stood up and tore his robe in grief. Then he shaved his head and fell to the ground to worship. He said, 'I came naked from my mother's womb, and I will be naked when I leave. The Lord gave me what I had, and the Lord has taken it away. Praise the name of the Lord!' In all of this, Job did not sin by blaming God."
~ Job 1:20-22 (NLT)

Job honestly acknowledged his pain and grief, yet exemplified faith. Despite all the things in his life taken away, Job praised the name of the Lord and did not blame God for any of the tragedies. He persevered and did not get angry with God.

Satan inflicted painful sores, from the soles of Job's feet to the top of his head, in another attempt to get Job to curse God.

"His wife said to him, 'Are you still maintaining your integrity? Curse God and die!' He replied, 'You are talking like a foolish woman. Shall we accept good from God, and not trouble?' In all this, Job did not sin in what he said."
~ Job 2:9-10

Even Job's wife believed Job should curse God. Job stood firm in his faith, knowing God was with him through the good and the bad. Under no circumstance would Job give in and curse God.

Three of Job's friends told him he was suffering because of sin or evil in his life. Job remained steadfast in his resolve to God. Job knew God was in charge, despite the tragedies.

"At last Job spoke, and he cursed the day of his birth. He said: 'Let the day of my birth be erased, and the night I was conceived.'"
~ Job 3:1-3 (NLT)

Job sank a bit into despondency listening to his friends, but Job refused to curse God. Instead, he cursed the day of his birth. He reasoned that the bad things that happened were God's will. God was still faithful and good.

The ending chapters of Job are conversations between God and Job, occurring in a storm. Through this, Job experienced God's presence in his suffering. Ultimately, God blessed the latter part of Job's life even more than the first because of his faithfulness.

"Then Job replied to the Lord: 'I know that you can do all things; no purpose of yours can be thwarted.' 'My ears had heard of you but now my eyes have seen you. Therefore I despise myself and repent in dust and ashes.'"
~ Job 42:1-2, 5-6

Job remained faithful and trusted God. Not once did he blame God for the bad. Job's faith was in God, whom he knew had the power to do anything and everything. He shows us how to persevere through any tragedy, knowing that everything works for the good of God.

Did you notice Job didn't ask:

Why the tragedies were happening?

Job modeled:

What can I do with this tragedy?
How can I glorify you, God, in this difficulty?

May these lessons from Job's life be a source of encouragement for us to…

live with integrity, knowing that God is working in every situation, whether it is good or bad.
acknowledge the tragedies in our lives, rather than pretending they aren't there.

try praising the Lord and not blaming Him for the tragedies.

know God is present in both the good and the bad.

not curse God for what happens in life.

look for God's presence in the storms of life.

know that God's purposes always prevail.

remain steadfast in faith and trust in the Lord.

focus on "What can I do with this tragedy?" and "How can I glorify God?"

REFLECTION:

Who are the people who speak life into your spirit?

When was a difficult time you asked God to help you glorify Him?

"Therefore, since we have been justified through faith, we have peace with God through our Lord Jesus Christ, through whom we have gained access by faith into this grace in which we now stand. And we boast in the hope of the glory of God. Not only so, but we also glory in our sufferings, because we know that suffering produces perseverance."

~ Romans 5:1-3

Christine M. Fisher

83

Resurrection

The resurrection of Jesus three days after His crucifixion is the pinnacle of our faith. In the last few years, I have come to realize even more the sacredness of the resurrection of Christ. Living in the time we do, we have the advantage of seeing the bigger picture, which helps our understanding of the saving power of Jesus.

The Bible and historical documents provide us with eyewitnesses who saw and recorded Jesus being put to death on a cross, buried, and resurrected. Eyewitnesses, including the disciples and some women like Mary Magdalene, shared time with the risen Jesus for another forty days after they found the tomb empty. It was then that Jesus ascended into heaven to sit at the right hand of God, His and our Father. Isn't it incredible to reflect on that, giving our faith a big boost?

> *"Early on Sunday morning, while it was still dark, Mary Magdalene came to the tomb and found that the stone had been rolled away from the entrance. She ran and found Simon Peter and the other disciple, the one whom Jesus loved. She said, 'They have taken the Lord's body out of the tomb, and we don't know where they have put him!' Peter and the other disciple started out for the tomb. They were both running, but the other disciple outran Peter and reached the tomb first. He stooped and looked in and saw the linen wrappings lying there, but he didn't go in. Then Simon Peter arrived and went inside. He also noticed the linen wrappings lying there, while the cloth that had covered Jesus' head was folded up and lying apart from the other wrappings. Then the disciple who had reached the tomb first also went in, and he saw*

and believed—for until then they still hadn't understood the Scriptures
that said Jesus must rise from the dead. Then they went home."
~ John 20:1-10 (NLT)

The eyewitnesses shared the detail that *"the cloth that had been wrapped around Jesus' head was still lying in its place."* This detail was given to us so that we indeed know Jesus resurrected from the dead. If someone had stolen Jesus' body from the tomb, most likely the cloth would not have been folded up in the same spot.

I read a commentary that shared an interesting Hebrew tradition from Jesus' day. The servant set the table for their master and hid just out of sight while the master was eating. When the master finished eating, he would wad up his napkin and throw it on the table, meaning "I'm finished." If the master got up from the table and folded the napkin, returning it next to his plate, it meant "I'm coming back." What a beautiful parallel with Jesus leaving us a folded cloth in the empty tomb.

How does the folded cloth in the tomb, representing "I'm coming back," encourage you to share your faith?

"Mary was standing outside the tomb crying, and as she wept, she stooped and looked in. She saw two white-robed angels, one sitting at the head and the other at the foot of the place where the body of Jesus had been lying. 'Dear woman, why are you crying?' the angels asked her. 'Because they have taken away my Lord,' she replied, 'and I don't know where they have put him.' She turned to leave and saw someone standing there. It was Jesus, but she didn't recognize him. 'Dear woman, why are you crying?' Jesus asked her. 'Who are you looking for?' She thought he was the gardener. 'Sir,' she said, 'if you have taken him away, tell me where you have put him, and I will go and get him.' 'Mary!' Jesus said. She turned to him and cried out, 'Rabboni!' (which is Hebrew for 'Teacher'). 'Don't cling to me,'" Jesus said, 'for I haven't yet ascended to the Father. But go

Christine M. Fisher

*find my brothers and tell them, "I am ascending to my Father and your
Father, to my God and your God."' Mary Magdalene found the disciples
and told them, 'I have seen the Lord!' Then she gave them his message."*
~ John 20:11-18 (NLT)

Mary Magdalene became a devout follower of Jesus after He delivered
her of seven demons. She was also present at Jesus' crucifixion and
burial, as well as being the first person to discover the empty tomb. At
the tomb, Mary Magdalene thought she was talking with the gardener,
but as soon as Jesus said "Mary," she recognized that it was Jesus in His
resurrected state. There is truth that the sheep recognizes the shepherd's
voice. Jesus met Mary right where she was that day when she was seeking
to find Him.

Do you hear Jesus calling your name as He meets you right where you are
while seeking Him with your heart?

> *"That Sunday evening the disciples were meeting behind locked doors
> because they were afraid of the Jewish leaders. Suddenly, Jesus was
> standing there among them! 'Peace be with you,' he said. As he spoke,
> he showed them the wounds in his hands and his side. They were filled
> with joy when they saw the Lord! Again he said, 'Peace be with you.
> As the Father has sent me, so I am sending you.' Then he breathed on
> them and said, 'Receive the Holy Spirit. If you forgive anyone's sins,
> they are forgiven. If you do not forgive them, they are not forgiven.'"*
> ~ John 20:19-23 (NLT)

God chose to have Jesus' resurrected state be such that His wounds
remained. I find it powerful to once again show the validity of the
resurrection. In their fear, Jesus appears for the first time to His disciples,
bringing them peace. Jesus does not give us a spirit of fear but rather one
of peace and joy, even in difficult circumstances. It was a powerful act that
Jesus breathed on them, sharing the gift of the Holy Spirit promised them.

Are you filled with peace and joy as Jesus breathes the Holy Spirit into your spirit?

Be encouraged to…

> share the resurrected Jesus with others.
> listen to Jesus calling your name and guiding you.
> let go of fear, letting the Risen Jesus fill you with peace and joy.

REFLECTION:

In what specific way can you share the resurrected Jesus with someone today?
What fear do you need to let go of?

"He was chosen before the creation of the world, but was revealed in these last times for your sake. Through him you believe in God, who raised him from the dead and glorified him, and so your faith and hope are in God."
~ 1 Peter 1:20-21

84

The Vision

One day, as I was feeling alone, I had a vision where I saw myself sitting outside, in the middle of a huge park. It was a beautiful, crystal-clear day, and a soft, gentle breeze was blowing. People were scurrying all about, but nobody seemed to notice me as I sat all alone. I couldn't believe my eyes, as suddenly, one by one, **things** began to disappear. First the trees, then the birds, and then the mountains. Houses once seen in the distance were erased from existence. Cars and buses were next; they were no longer to be found. Lastly, the people, one by one, disappeared—no more family, friends, or strangers around. All the places where I had once seen God's beauty suddenly vanished.

As I looked around once more, there was only me and nothing else. But, within my heart and soul, I had an unexplainable peace. I knew in my heart that, although all the **things** of this world were taken away, I still had **something**. You see, I was not alone—I had **Jesus** living in my heart—a treasure far greater than anything on earth. It was then that I realized the true meaning of life.

REFLECTION:

Does knowing that Jesus, your greatest treasure, is always with you bring you comfort?
When have you experienced the peace that surpasses all understanding?

> *"Suddenly a great company of the heavenly host appeared*
> *with the angel, praising God and saying,*
> *'Glory to God in the highest heaven, and on earth*
> *peace to those on whom his favor rests.'"*
> ~ Luke 2:13-14

85

The Lord's Prayer

A friend reminded me of this simple yet powerful thought. It is something I find myself repeating frequently, along with thanking God for providing.

"Give us today our daily bread."
~ Matthew 6:11

I am sure you recognize this line from the Lord's Prayer found in the gospels of Matthew and Luke.

"One day Jesus was praying in a certain place. When he finished, one of his disciples said to him, 'Lord, teach us to pray, just as John taught his disciples.' He said to them, 'When you pray, say: "Father, hallowed is your name, your kingdom come. Give us each day our daily bread. Forgive us our sins, for we also forgive everyone who sins against us. And lead us not into temptation."'"
~ Luke 11:1-4

It fascinates me how many times the Bible mentions Jesus going off by Himself to pray. If Jesus, being God's Son, took so much time to be alone with God and pray, how much more praying should we be doing? What a great example He left for us to imitate. I like, too, that the disciples wanted to know **how** Jesus prayed.

"And when you pray, do not be like the hypocrites, for they love to pray standing in the synagogues and on the street corners to be seen by others. Truly I tell you, they have received their reward in full. But when you pray, go into your room, close the door and pray to your Father, who is unseen. Then your Father, who sees what is done in secret, will reward

you. And when you pray, do not keep on babbling like pagans, for they
think they will be heard because of their many words. Do not be like
them, for your Father knows what you need before you ask him."
~ Matthew 6:5-8

From Matthew's introduction to the Lord's Prayer, we learn how we should pray. Our hearts need to be sincere in our love for God. We should not pray on the street corners for others to think we are pious, as then our hearts are not right with God. Jesus tells us we do not need to use many words to get God's attention. God listens to the sincerity of our prayers and knows all our needs. When we pray from our hearts, we enter God's presence and experience a personal encounter with Him.

"This, then, is how you should pray:
'Our Father in heaven,
hallowed by your name,
your kingdom come,
your will be done, on earth as it is in heaven.
Give us today our daily bread.
And forgive us our debts,
as we also have forgiven our debtors.
And lead us not into temptation,
but deliver us from the evil one.'"
~ Matthew 6:9-13

Let's look at the meaning of each of the lines in the Lord's Prayer:

"Our Father in heaven..."
We acknowledge that God is our true Father, who is in heaven.

"hallowed be your name..."
We give praise to God, for His name is holy.

"your kingdom come..."

> We ask for God's kingdom to reign in our lives.

"your will be done, on earth as it is in heaven."

> We pray God's divine will be done on this earth, just as it is in heaven.

"Give us today our daily bread..."

> We take one day at a time, knowing God provides everything we need when we need it.

"and forgive us our debts..."

> We need to recognize we are sinners and seek reconciliation in Jesus.

"as we also have forgiven our debtors."

> Since God has forgiven us through Jesus, we need to forgive those who have wronged us too.

"And lead us not into temptation..."

> We need to pray to resist temptation in our lives so we remain close to God.

"but deliver us from the evil one."

> Praying to be rescued from Satan is necessary. We belong to God, and God alone.

May you be inspired to pray the Lord's Prayer daily remembering...

> God is our Father.
> to praise God.
> to desire God's kingdom on this earth.
> to line up your will with God's.
> to see how God provides what you need each day.

to seek and share God's forgiveness.

with God's help, you can avoid temptation and Satan.

I will continue to repeat and reflect on *"Give us today our daily bread,"* knowing God provides everything I need at the exact moment I need it, one day at a time.

REFLECTION:

Do you need to slow down a little and take time to be in God's presence? What verse in the Lord's Prayer speaks to your heart most and serves as a good reminder?

"The Son is the radiance of God's glory and the exact representation of his being, sustaining all things by his powerful word. After he had provided purification for sins, he sat down at the right hand of the Majesty in heaven."
~ Hebrews 1:3

86

Obedient Growth

One January day, while running errands, I saw an incoming email with the title "Guest Speaker," sent from someone I did not know. Somehow, I knew it was a request for a speaking engagement, completely outside my comfort zone. But, as an introverted yet obedient writer, my attitude was, "Okay, Lord. I know you are bringing this to me, so I will do it." That attitude alone is progress for me.

This was my first endeavor to write a talk, not exclusively related to my writing journey, for an event scheduled in April for a Ladies of Charity Morning of Reflection. When I learned about this organization, whose motto is to serve, not be served, and the different guiding principles of their ministry, I knew the best thing would be to encourage them. I was reminded of the similarities with Jesus' three years of ministry. After I penned the rough draft, a friend gave me a few thoughts on improving it. Running the final copy by another person gave me confidence to trust that it was what the Lord intended to be shared.

As I was driving to the venue, I thought about the thoughts Jesus must have experienced on his walk to Calvary, wondering if I was possibly experiencing some of those same thoughts.

Jesus Knew His Time had come to Surrender His Life.

> "When Jesus had finished saying all these things, he said to his disciples, 'As you know, the Passover is two days away—and the Son of Man will be handed over to be crucified.'"
> ~ Matthew 26:1-2

Christine M. Fisher

Jesus shared with His disciples, even two days before the Passover that the time was coming soon for Him to fulfill God's will of being the Savior of the world. He walked in confidence, knowing the timing was divinely orchestrated.

I, too, knew my time had come to step out in faith, knowing I was ready to do God's will by sharing with these ladies. It brought me a sense of confidence and a place of peaceful surrender, knowing I was being obedient.

JESUS KNEW THERE WAS POWER IN PRAYER.

> *"Then Jesus went with his disciples to a place called Gethsemane,*
> *and he said to them, 'Sit here while I go over there and pray.'"*
> ~ Matthew 26:36

> *"He went away a second time and prayed, 'My Father, if it is not possible*
> *for this cup to be taken away unless I drink it, may your will be done.'"*
> ~ Matthew 26:42

Jesus often went off by Himself to pray. He needed continual communion with His Father. Jesus was honest with God, wanting the Father's will to be done no matter how painful. He knew He could endure anything with God's help.

A little before my reflection began, a lady told me that she had been lifting me up in prayer. She knew how difficult it was to talk in front of a group of people, as she has done so often throughout the years. It brought comfort to know she had been praying specifically for me.

JESUS KNEW HIS FATHER WAS ACCOMPANYING HIM THROUGH EVERYTHING.

> *"'Now we can see that you know all things and that you do not even need*
> *to have anyone ask you questions. This makes us believe that you came*
> *from God.' 'Do you now believe?' Jesus replied. 'A time is coming and in*

fact has come when you will be scattered, each to your own home. You will leave me all alone. Yet I am not alone, for my Father is with me. I have told you these things, so that in me you may have peace. In this world you will have trouble. But take heart! I have overcome the world.'"
~ John 16:30-33

Jesus knew ...

> He was one with the Father,
> Judas would betray Him, and
> Peter would deny Him.
>
> the disciples would fall asleep while He was fervently praying.
> humans would desert Him, but
> His Father in heaven would accompany Him each step of the way.

Jesus came to bring peace despite the troubles of this world.

On my way to the event, I knew God was with me, giving me the power and strength I needed. God never leaves us and He provides what we need when we need it. Throughout the event, I experienced the peace of Jesus.

Jesus Knew There was Peace and Joy in Obedience to God's Will.

> *"We do this by keeping our eyes on Jesus, the champion who initiates and perfects our faith. Because of the joy awaiting him, he endured the cross, disregarding its shame. Now he is seated in the place of honor beside God's throne."*
> ~ Hebrews 12:2 (NLT)

Jesus willingly endured the agony of the cross, which was a sign of shame and wrongdoing, but Jesus turned the cross into victory. The cross grants us the gift of eternal life because of Jesus' obedience in doing God's

Christine M. Fisher

will. What peace and joy must have filled Jesus, especially when He was reunited in heaven with God.

My heart was filled with peace and joy throughout my time with the Ladies of Charity. I was blessed to meet some who said they read my weekly reflections or had one of my books. It was good to speak and share about God's goodness.

Be encouraged to…

> surrender your life to God.
> know the power of prayer.
> know God is accompanying you each step of the way.
> live in peace and joy while being obedient to God's will.

REFLECTION:

When did you step out in obedience and faith to do something difficult? Have you experienced joy and peace when doing something outside of your comfort zone?

> *"Then he said to them all: 'Whoever wants to be my disciple must deny themselves and take up their cross daily and follow me. For whoever wants to save their life will lose it, but whoever loses their life for me will save it. What good is it for someone to gain the whole world, and yet lose or forfeit their very self? Whoever is ashamed of me and my words, the Son of Man will be ashamed of them when he comes in his glory and in the glory of the Father and of the holy angels.'"*
> ~ Luke 9:23-26

87

September Reflections

September is the month God planned for me to make my entrance into this world. In His infinite goodness, God created me and fashioned me in my mother's womb. I have been blessed to know the Lord throughout my life and have felt the most growth in my relationship with Him during the last few years. His presence has taken on a deeper meaning, and I have experienced His love in the ways He reveals Himself to me.

> *"Mordecai sent this reply to Esther: 'Don't think for a moment that because you're in the palace you will escape when all other Jews are killed. If you keep quiet at a time like this, deliverance and relief for the Jews will arise from some other place, but you and your relatives will die. Who knows if perhaps you were made queen for just such a time as this?'"*
> ~ Esther 4:13-14 (NLT)

Esther realized she had a big decision to make. God's sovereign will would be carried out, but would it be through her? If she took personal responsibility, she, along with her family, would be saved in addition to the Jews. God quite possibly made her queen for that purpose. Thankfully, she followed God's sovereign will, something we all should try to do. I pray my life may always follow God's lead.

On September 5, 2014, I published my first weekly reflection on sharing God in the ordinary of life. I set out to see if God would inspire me to pen weekly thoughts on a website, and I can attest to God's faithfulness in accomplishing that task for His glory.

Christine M. Fisher

These years have been a great adventure of trusting God and growing through seeing Him at work in my life. He is molding and shaping me into the person He wants, which is a great feeling.

How fitting to share this thought from a friend:

> "God made you who you are,
> and placed you where you are,
> because where you are,
> needs who you are."

Yes, God...

made you.
placed you right where you are.
needs you where you are.

No matter where you are...

God has you right where you are supposed to be.
God's presence is with you.
God has specific plans for your life.

The Scripture story of Jesus walking on the water confirms the above quote.

> *"Immediately Jesus made the disciples get into the boat and go on ahead of him to the other side, while he dismissed the crowd. After he had dismissed them, he went up on a mountainside by himself to pray. Later that night, he was there alone, and the boat was already a considerable distance from land, buffeted by the waves because the wind was against it. Shortly before dawn Jesus went out to them, walking on the lake. When the disciples saw him walking on the lake, they were terrified. 'It's a ghost,' they said, and cried*

out in fear. But Jesus immediately said to them: 'Take courage! It is I. Don't be afraid.' 'Lord, if it's you,' Peter replied, 'tell me to come to you on the water.' 'Come,' he said. Then Peter got down out of the boat, walked on the water and came toward Jesus. But when he saw the wind, he was afraid and, beginning to sink, cried out, 'Lord, save me!' Immediately Jesus reached out his hand and caught him. 'You of little faith,' he said, 'why did you doubt?'"
~ Matthew 14:22-31

Jesus made the disciples get into the boat.

They were right where He wanted them.

"Take courage! It is I. Don't be afraid." "Come," he said.

Jesus reassured Peter of His presence, which was leading and guiding him.

Immediately, Jesus reached out His hand and caught Peter.

Jesus is always reaching for our hand to lead us and catch us if we start to fall.

You are unique, and nobody else can carry out the mission God has planned for you.

Glorify God and know that your life is an essential part of the kingdom of God.

God has great plans for your life.

Keep being obedient to Him day by day as He leads you.

REFLECTION:

What is one way God is glorified in your life?

How have you walked in obedience, letting God lead?

"May all the kings of the earth praise you, Lord,
when they hear what you have decreed.
May they sing of the ways of the Lord, for the glory of the Lord is great."
~ Psalm 138:4-5

88

The Face of Jesus

I received a text from a deacon who ministers five days a week at a nursing home. He shares Scripture, reflections, prayer, songs, and God's love. The nursing home houses people who have either dementia or Alzheimer's. I enjoy hearing his stories of how God works through him to minister to the residents.

He shared how amazing it is when he starts to say The Lord's Prayer and they all join in. The same is true with some songs he sings with them, like *He's Got the Whole World in His Hands.* Isn't it inspiring to know they can recall some of the most important things, like God's Word?

His text said,

"I see the face of Jesus in the nursing home residents."

His words were powerful. Since we are made in God's image and have the Holy Spirit within us, shouldn't we see the face of Jesus reflected in people? But how many times do we see the face of Jesus in others? Do we take time to even think about it or bother to look?

Do we see the face of Jesus in the...

> boss or coworker who is difficult to work with?
> spouse who brings you flowers to brighten your day?
> elderly person in a nursing home?
> person waiting on you at the restaurant?
> doctor who gives you a bad report?
> person who listens to you with their heart?

Christine M. Fisher

person who has no money for food?

friend who offers you words of encouragement?

homeless person who has nothing?

pastor who shares God's word?

lonely, forgotten person in jail?

child who needs someone to care about them as they find their way?

person going through cancer treatments?

child you sponsor from a Third World country?

person who looks different because of a physical ailment?

drug addict you pass on the street?

"For I was hungry and you gave me food, I was thirsty and you gave me drink, I was a stranger and you welcomed me, I was naked and you clothed me, I was sick and you visited me, I was in prison and you came to me. Then the righteous will answer him, saying, 'Lord, when did we see you hungry and feed you, or thirsty and give you drink? And when did we see you a stranger and welcome you, or naked and clothe you? And when did we see you sick or in prison and visit you?' And the King will answer them, 'Truly, I say to you, as you did it to one of the least of these my brothers, you did it to me.'"
~ Matthew 25:35-40 (ESV)

When we provide for others in their time of need, we are doing it for Jesus. Knowing that, shouldn't we see the face of Jesus in those people? Isn't that something special to consider? We are able to share and reflect the caring and compassionate lifestyle of Jesus with others. We know the sanctity and value of every human life. God made each of us beautiful, worthy, precious, and loveable. Bringing that to life in others through our actions is a great mission.

"Keep on loving each other as brothers and sisters. Don't forget to show hospitality to strangers, for some who have done this have entertained angels without realizing it! Remember those in

prison, as if you were there yourself. Remember also those being
mistreated, as if you felt their pain in your own bodies."
~ Hebrews 13:1-3 (NLT)

God is love. Jesus came to earth and shared love with everyone; He reached out to the marginalized and the forgotten. We have the mission to follow in Jesus' footsteps through sharing His love, concern for others, and realizing the dignity of everyone. If we are sharing Christ's love, we can't help but see the face of Christ in our brothers and sisters and in everyone we meet.

Do we see the face of Jesus in…

> the person who no longer speaks to us?
> the person who cut us off in traffic?
> the person who harmed us?

How can we be encouraged to see the face of Jesus in these people?

By remembering…

> to pray for our enemies.
> to want the best for everyone.
> that Jesus died for them.
> they might have a deep wound that needs to be healed.
> to look for something positive in them.
> they, too, are children of God.

Can you recall a special time when you saw the face of Jesus in a powerful way?

I saw His face in a lady who was trying to remove the snow and ice from around her mailbox. As I drove by, our eyes connected, and I saw her look of desperation, which reminded me of the agony Jesus endured on His way to Calvary. This prompted me to forego my errands, go home and pick up my son and take a few shovels to help her. She was appreciative and, from that encounter, we have engaged in more conversations over the years.

I have seen the face of Jesus through interactions with a pastor at church, as the face of Jesus pierced my heart and soul, and I experienced His immense love and compassion for me. I felt Jesus' pure and unconditional love—a vulnerability letting Him into my heart—which brought me to tears in His presence.

May you be encouraged to…

> see the face of Jesus in everyone, even the difficult people in your life.
> reflect on and give thanks for a time you encountered seeing the face of Jesus.

REFLECTION:

When have you experienced seeing the face of Jesus in someone?
When did you see the face of Jesus touch your spirit?

> *"Glory in his holy name; let the hearts of those who seek the Lord rejoice. Look to the Lord and his strength; seek his face always."*
> ~ Psalm 105:3-4

89

The Kingdom of Heaven

What is the kingdom of heaven?

"In those days John the Baptist came, preaching in the wilderness of Judea and saying, 'Repent, for the kingdom of heaven has come near.' This is he who was spoken of through the prophet Isaiah: 'A voice of one calling in the wilderness, "Prepare the way for the Lord, make straight paths for him."'"
~ Matthew 3:1-3

Isaiah prophesied about both John the Baptist and Jesus. John would be the one calling in the wilderness, sharing the good news about the coming of the Lord Jesus. The kingdom of heaven drew near to us when God sent Jesus to be the Savior of the world. When we accept Jesus as our personal Lord and Savior, we belong to the kingdom of heaven.

What is the kingdom of heaven like?

Three of the four Gospel writers, Matthew, Mark, and Luke, share several parables about the kingdom of heaven. Christianity.com defines a parable as: "a simple story to provide a more profound lesson or teaching."

"He [Jesus] told them another parable: 'The kingdom of heaven is like a mustard seed, which a man took and planted in his field. Though it is the smallest of all seeds, yet when it grows, it is the largest of garden plants and becomes a tree, so that the birds come and perch in its branches.'"
~ Matthew 13:31-32

Christine M. Fisher

Imagine a mustard seed, one of the smallest of seeds. Yet Jesus says the seed grows into a garden plant and then becomes a huge tree. A mustard tree is as tall as it is wide, and the birds of the air come to rest in its branches. This parable teaches us that the kingdom of heaven may seem to start out small and insignificant, but eventually it will spread throughout the whole world. All nations will find rest in the kingdom.

Have you experienced planting a mustard seed of faith in someone that you watched grow into a mustard tree?

> *"He told them still another parable: 'The kingdom of heaven is like yeast that a woman took and mixed into about sixty pounds of flour until it worked all through the dough.'"*
> ~ Matthew 13:33

Consider how only a small amount of yeast is needed compared to a large amount of flour—sixty pounds, to be exact—to make bread. The yeast must be kneaded well throughout the flour in order to produce the proper growth. The kingdom of heaven is like yeast in our lives that produces growth in us to help us have a deeper relationship with the Spirit and draw others deeper into their relationship.

Who has been like yeast in your life, helping your faith grow deeper? Have you thanked them?

> *"'Again, the kingdom of heaven is like a merchant in search of fine pearls, who, on finding one pearl of great value, went and sold all that he had and bought it.'"*
> ~ Matthew 13:45-46 (ESV)

Can you see yourself as a merchant searching for the finest of pearls? You know there is great value in finding the perfect pearl and are willing to pay whatever the cost is. The kingdom of heaven is the finest of pearls we encounter on our journey. We should be willing to leave our life of sin and distance ourselves from others in order to gain the greatest pearl in life, the kingdom of heaven.

How can you share the pearl of the greatest value, Jesus, with someone today?

> *"The kingdom of heaven is like treasure hidden in a field,*
> *which a man found and covered up. Then in his joy he*
> *goes and sells all that he has and buys that field."*
> ~ Matthew 13:44 (ESV)

Imagine finding treasure hidden in a field. Back in Jesus' day, if people were trying to hide a treasure, they would bury it until they were able to safely secure it. The treasure had much value, so in their joy, they were willing to sell what they needed in order to obtain the treasure. When we discover the kingdom of heaven, we realize the value and treasure we have. We are overcome with joy and want to share it with others.

Take a few moments to thank Jesus for the treasure of the kingdom of heaven you experience daily.

Be encouraged to…

> plant a mustard seed of faith in someone.
> be the yeast in someone's life.
> have gratitude for the pearl of Jesus.
> share the joy of the greatest treasure of Jesus.

REFLECTION:

Who has helped plant mustard seeds of faith in your life?
Is there someone you are being nudged to share Jesus with?

"Yours, Lord, is the greatness and the power and the glory and the majesty and the splendor, for everything in heaven and earth is yours. Yours, Lord, is the kingdom; you are exalted as head over all. Wealth and honor come from you; you are the ruler of all things. In your hands are strength and power to exalt and give strength to all."
~ 1 Chronicles 29:11-12

90

Prism of Light

In optics, a prism is a transparent, solid body that disperses or reflects light. When white light, which is composed of the colors of a rainbow, passes through a prism, a spectrum of color is produced, spreading more light and beauty.

When I think about the word light, the first thing that comes to mind is how Jesus is the light of the world. How fitting that we celebrate Jesus' birth around the time of the darkest day of the year.

> *"In the beginning was the Word, and the Word was with God, and the Word was God. He was with God in the beginning. Through him all things were made; without him nothing was made that has been made. In him was life, and that life was the light of all mankind. The light shines in the darkness, and the darkness has not overcome it. The light shines in the darkness, and the darkness has not overcome it. There was a man sent from God whose name was John. He came as a witness to testify concerning that light, so that through him all might believe. He himself was not the light; he came only as a witness to the light. The true light that gives light to everyone was coming into the world."*
> ~ John 1:1-9

This Scripture passage is rich in meaning. The Word, Jesus, was present in the very beginning with God and was a part of God. Everything was made through Jesus, and in Him is life, which is light for all. Light triumphs over darkness. God sent John the Baptist to share the good news of Jesus, the light, so that all might believe in Him.

JESUS IS THE LIGHT.

"Arise, shine, for your light has come, and the glory of the Lord rises upon you. See, darkness covers the earth and thick darkness is over the peoples, but the Lord rises upon you and his glory appears over you. Nations will come to your light, and kings to the brightness of your dawn."
~ Isaiah 60:1-3

These verses were written before God sent Jesus to earth. The Lord is referred to as the light and the glory that have come to the people. Despite the gloom and darkness present, the Lord's light and glory are greater and have the victory. Nations and people are drawn to the light and glory of the Lord they see in us rather than being in darkness.

GOD'S GLORY SHINES IN THE DARKNESS.

"For you were once darkness, but now you are light in the Lord. Live as children of light (for the fruit of the light consists in all goodness, righteousness and truth.)"
~ Ephesians 5:8-9

In these verses, Paul, an apostle of Jesus, reminds us that we were once darkness, but now that we know Jesus, we are light. He encourages us to continually remain illuminated by the light, which will be reflected through the fruits of living a moral and ethical life.

WE ARE LIGHT.

When God sent Jesus to earth to be born of a woman, a great light appeared in the sky.

"After Jesus was born in Bethlehem in Judea, during the time of King Herod, Magi from the east came to Jerusalem and asked,

*'Where is the one who has been born king of the Jews? We saw
his star when it rose and have come to worship him.'"*
~ Matthew 2:1-2

*"After they had heard the king, they went on their way, and the star
they had seen when it rose went ahead of them until it stopped over the
place where the child was. When they saw the star, they were overjoyed.
On coming to the house, they saw the child with his mother Mary, and
they bowed down and worshipped him. Then they opened their treasures
and presented him with gifts of gold, frankincense and myrrh."*
~ Matthew 2:9-11

The Magi, who were probably astrologers, noticed a particularly bright light in the sky. They knew it was not an ordinary star and that it led to the king of the Jews, so they wanted to follow it. When they arrived, they were overjoyed to find Jesus. They bowed down and worshipped Him, knowing He would do great things.

What if we consider the star that led to Jesus, as well as Jesus Himself, as the white light shining through a prism? Jesus shares the glory of the Lord as the light passes through the prism. The light produces a glorious rainbow through the prism that touches all of us as we encounter Jesus. We come to know God's great love for us too.

Now view your life through a prism.

Does the light of Jesus' prism shine through your prism and disperse or reflect a beautiful rainbow into the lives of others?

Does the glory of God produce the light in your prism?

Be encouraged, knowing...

>Jesus is the light.
>God's glory shines in the darkness.
>we are the light.

>the star that leads to Jesus still shines brilliantly.
>Jesus is the glorious rainbow of God.
>your life disperses Jesus' light and God's glory to all.

Go, be the prism of light in your little corner of the world. May the beauty of the rainbow of Jesus' light radiate from you as you spread more light and beauty into the lives of all you encounter.

REFLECTION:

How have you dispersed Jesus' light to someone today?
Who has helped illuminate your path so you walk more faithfully?

>*"Then your light will break forth like the dawn, and your*
>*healing will quickly appear; then your righteousness will go before*
>*you, and the glory of the Lord will be your rear guard."*
>~ Isaiah 58:8

CONCLUSION

I hope exploring glimpses of God's glory through these 90 devotions has helped you see even more of God's manifested presence in your life and in the world. God is amazing. His glory is never-ending and is always around and in us. I pray your spiritual eyes continue to see God's glory everywhere, every day. May you share that with others to help them see it too. God's glory is manifested in nature, in people, and in Jesus.

I will leave you with this reflection as you keep in mind: we are made in God's image and have the privilege of living consciously for His glory.

The Mission of My Life

"God has created me to do Him some definite service. He has committed some work to me which He has not committed to another. I have my mission. I may never know it in this life, but I shall be told it in the next. I am a link in a chain, a bond of connection between persons. He has not created me for naught. I shall do good; I shall do His work. I shall be an angel of peace, a preacher of truth in my own place, while not intending it if I do but keep His commandments. Therefore, I will trust Him, whatever I am, I can never be thrown away. If I am in sickness, my sickness may serve Him, in perplexity, my perplexity may serve Him. If I am in sorrow, my sorrow may serve Him. He does nothing in vain. He knows what He is about. He may take away my friends. He may throw

me among strangers. He may make me feel desolate, make my spirits sink, hide my future from me. Still, He knows what He is about."
~ St. John Henry Newman

"And they were calling to one another: 'Holy, holy, holy is the Lord Almighty; the whole earth is full of his glory.'"
~ Isaiah 6:3

ABOUT THE AUTHOR

Christine Fisher is a simple, ordinary gal, a child of God, a lover of Jesus, a daughter, wife and mother. She models her life after the ministry of Jesus Christ, serving and encouraging the lonely, the homeless, and the hurting. Through writing, Christine shares God's presence, goodness, and grace through the ordinary things in life. She enjoys spending quiet time in nature worshiping the Creator. Christine and her husband, Mark, live in upstate New York.

"Publish his glorious deeds among the nations.
Tell everyone about the amazing things he does."
~ 1 Chronicles 16:24 (NLT)

"One generation commends your works to another; they tell of your
mighty acts. They speak of the glorious splendor of your majesty—and
I will meditate on your wonderful works. They tell of the power of your
awesome works—and I will proclaim your great deeds. They celebrate
your abundant goodness and joyfully sing of your righteousness."
~ Psalm 145:4-7

NOTES

Day 24: The Pearl

1   Annie: *Something Was Missing* lyrics © Edwin H. Morris & Co. Inc., Strada Music, Morris-edwin-h-co Inc., Charles Strouse Publishing, Strada-music Co. Songwriters: Martin Charnin / Charles Strouse. 1972.

Day 65: There is Hope

2   *Cry Out To Jesus*, Wherever You Are, Third Day, Released 2005.

Day 68: Jesus' Presence

3   Andrew Lloyd-Webber / Richard Stillgoe / Charles Hart; *All I Ask of You*, September 1986, Andrew Lloyd Webber

4   ibid.